THE FRENCH AND INDIAN WARS

BRITISH MUSEUM

The French and Indian Wars

BY THE EDITORS OF
AMERICAN HERITAGE
The Magazine of History

AUTHOR
FRANCIS RUSSELL

CONSULTANT
LAWRENCE HENRY GIPSON
Author of *The British Empire Before
the American Revolution*

*Illustrated with Paintings, Prints, Engravings,
and Maps, Many of the Period*

PERENNIAL ♛ LIBRARY

Harper & Row, Publishers
NEW YORK AND EVANSTON

ACKNOWLEDGMENTS

The Editors are especially indebted to the following individuals for their generous assistance and advice in preparing this book: Mrs. I. M. B. Dobell, Curator of the McCord Museum, McGill University, Montreal; Georges Delisle, Chief of the Picture Division, Public Archives of Canada, Ottawa; F. St. George Spendlove, Curator of the Canadiana Collections, Sigmund Samuel Canadiana Gallery, Royal Ontario Museum, Toronto; George MacBeath, Curator of Canadian History, New Brunswick Museum, Saint John; and Mrs. Thomas V. Lape, Librarian of the Fort Ticonderoga Museum, Ticonderoga, New York. The Glens Falls Insurance Company granted special permission to reproduce the painting on pages 98–99. Thanks are also due the following persons and organizations for their assistance: The John Carter Brown Library, Brown University, Providence—Thomas R. Adams; New-York Historical Society, New York City—Paul Bride; Edward E. Ayer Collection, Newberry Library, Chicago—Colton Storm; Mrs. John Nicholas Brown, Providence; The National Gallery of Canada, Ottawa— J. Russell Harper; Wisconsin State Historical Society, Madison— Paul Vanderbilt; State Education Department of New York, Albany—Wallace F. Workmaster; Provincial Archives of Quebec, Quebec—Antoine Roy; Trinity Church of Saint John, New Brunswick—Christina Hawkins; Onondaga Historical Association, Syracuse—Richard N. Wright; Warner House Association, Portsmouth, N.H.—Col. Henry B. Margeson; Pocumtuck Valley Memorial Association, Deerfield, Mass.—Henry Flynt.

For this edition selective details have been taken from certain paintings that were reproduced in full in the original edition. Such details appear on pages 5, 8, 16-17, 21, 24 (William III), 64 (both), 72-73, 74, 79 (Capt. Orme), 102, 105, 110, 112 (both), 118-119, 124.

THE FRENCH AND INDIAN WARS *was originally published by American Heritage Publishing Co., Inc., in 1962. The Perennial Library edition is published by arrangement with American Heritage. It reproduces the complete text and selected illustrations from the American Heritage edition. First Perennial Library edition published 1965 by Harper & Row, Publishers, Incorporated, New York and Evanston.*

LIBRARY OF CONGRESS CATALOG CARD NUMBER: 62–15314

Foreword

In the colonization of North America the Spaniards, the French, the Dutch, the Swedes, and the English, in turn, each sought a share. The Spaniards fastened upon Florida and Mexico, but their efforts to expand further came to a halt, and in the course of time the Dutch and the Swedish holdings along the Atlantic seaboard fell to the English. Only Great Britain and France remained as rivals for the heart of the continent.

At first there was little contact between the two, since their settlements were widely separated by a vast and forbidding wilderness. Engrossed in their struggle to gain a livelihood, the English and French settlers might long have remained at peace. But the parent countries became engaged in hostilities which inevitably involved their New World colonies.

Three times, beginning in 1690, warfare flamed in the no man's land between New France and New England. Settlements were destroyed and armies clashed in the wilderness, yet nothing was settled. After the Peace of Aix-la-Chapelle, in 1748, all attempts to reach agreement over rival North American territorial claims failed. The use of force was the final resort. Each nation regarded the Ohio Valley as its own. A mere skirmish occurred there in 1754, but it touched off a war that spread to Europe, then to Africa, Asia, and even to islands in the Atlantic and Pacific. It was fought with bitter determination for nine years on land and sea, with the fate of North America hanging in the balance. This conflict, the Great War for the Empire, may well be called the first of the world wars.

These four wars of rivalry for possession of the Ohio Valley and other wilderness lands are the subject of Mr. Russell's book. The maps, prints, and other contemporary pictures bring to life the vast panorama that formed the background for this struggle in which English redcoats fought side by side with American colonists against the dashing French and their tomahawk-wielding Indian allies.

Little did the victorious British realize in 1763—upon the signing of the treaty of peace terminating the Great War for the Empire—that all too soon their empire would be greatly reduced in size. The thirteen American colonies emerged from the war mature, both economically and politically, and possessing thousands of battle-hardened veterans. With the French threat now removed from North America, they no longer felt the need of the mother country's protection. This feeling of self-reliance stemming from the French and Indian Wars was to become one of the most important factors leading to the American Revolution.

LAWRENCE HENRY GIPSON

HALF TITLE: *The British grenadier in these sketches, from a 1744 training manual, displays the proper way to throw his specialty, the hand grenade.*

FOREWORD: *Ruthlessly killing and burning, Frenchmen and Indians overwhelmed the Massachusetts settlement of Deerfield in 1704, during Queen Anne's War.*

Contents

1.

The Battleground

THE TINY PALISADED settlement of Schenectady, New York, lay still and sleeping under a heavy blanket of snow. It was a bitterly cold February night in the year 1690. The villagers had been warned that a marauding band of Frenchmen and Indians from Canada was in the vicinity, but the warning had been ignored. The gates in the log wall were open, and only a pair of snow men stood watch—the garrison of twenty-four militiamen was asleep.

Shortly after midnight, shadows flickered across the snow. Figures materialized at the gates and slipped inside, silently making their way among the houses until every one was surrounded. A war whoop split the frosty air; hardly had the sound stopped echoing in the ears of the drowsy inhabitants before the doors were driven in, and knife and tomahawk followed. The garrison, belatedly alert, perished to a man as the town blazed. Thirty-eight men and boys died in that night of terror, and twenty-two women and children. Only two Frenchmen were killed. Early next morning the attackers slipped away, carrying off twenty-seven prisoners and leaving behind blood-stained, smoking ruins. They marched toward Montreal, two hundred miles to the north, and the white cold of the northern winter swallowed them up as silently as they had come.

The Schenectady massacre was the opening act of a great conflict that ran its bitter and bloody course through North America for seventy years. From 1690 to 1760 this conflict, the French and Indian Wars, blew

---

The bloody nighttime raid by the French and Indians on Schenectady, New York, in 1690, marked the beginning of the grim seventy-year struggle between the English and the French for North America. Men, women, and children were killed and scalped; even dogs and cattle were butchered.

9

sometimes hot, sometimes warm, but almost never cold. It was a war more savage than any practiced in Europe, one in which the victor stood to win a continent.

In Europe in the seventeenth and eighteenth centuries, kings joined or opposed other kings and started their wars over who should sit on the throne of Spain or Austria or inherit the Lowlands or the banks of the Rhine. Such wars were fought by soldiers drilled so rigidly that they seemed clockwork men in uniform, to be wound up and sent moving in straight lines toward each other across flat fields. Nobody fought in the wintertime, and one big battle every other year was considered quite enough. The officers on both sides were gentlemen, and they understood each other. War was the most dangerous of games, yet it was a game with fixed rules. It was against the rules, for example, to surrender a fortress until a breach had been made in the walls large enough to drive a gun carriage through.

For England there was always the stern problem of the balance of power, of preventing any one country from dominating the Continent. So England, with varying allies, fought successively against France in the War of the Grand Alliance (1689–1697), the War of the Spanish Succession (1701–1714), the War of the Austrian Succession (1740–1748), and the Great War for the Empire (1754–1763).

In America these wars were called King William's War, Queen Anne's War, King George's War, and the French and Indian War. The final war gave its name to the whole seventy-year period of conflict in the New World; each was no more than a campaign in one great war between the English and the French for North America.

If the European phases of this world-wide struggle

were commanded by gentlemen and fought according to fixed rules, the soldiers in the ranks were not gentlemen—in fact, they were scarcely regarded as human beings. Criminals or derelicts scraped out of the gutter, or farm boys impressed against their will, they were molded by a harsh, iron discipline. The goal of the drillmasters was to create a soldier who, without faltering, would march up to the muzzle of an enemy gun. Steps measured to drumbeat, two symmetrical lines of infantry—in pipe-clayed breeches, blue or green or white or red coats, powdered hair queued back under peaked brass helmets—would advance to within a few dozen yards of each other and fire point-blank.

At the Battle of Fontenoy in Belgium in 1745, as the French and the English infantry moved relentlessly toward each other, a young captain of the Grenadier Guards, Lord Charles Hay, marched out ahead of his men. Only a few yards from the French line he bowed, drank a toast from his flask, and called out, "Gentlemen of France, fire first!"

Lord Hay could not have made his gallant gesture in the New World. Advancing alone, he would have heard a war whoop and been scalped, or a marksman in the underbrush would have picked him off. Yet, often, European generals crossing the Atlantic could not grasp the idea that a battle might be fought in ways other than the slow advance of rigid ranks across a Flanders plain. For this they had been trained; this was the way it ought to be done—not with undisciplined militia in homespun and half-naked savages. In their contempt, marshals and generals with proud names and proud regiments often bred their own destruction.

Ever since their arrival in North America, the French and English had been at odds. Their opposing ways of life, their religion and their habits, set them naturally

against one another. The French had come to trade for furs and to convert the Indians, and as they set up their little posts around the Great Lakes and down the Mississippi Valley, they began to conceive of a mighty empire of New France. The English were not interested in converting the Indians but in getting rid of them, and although some were traders, most had come to get away from an empire rather than to found one. They built compact communities of fishermen and farmers along the eastern seacoast. By the middle of the eighteenth century there were almost a million transplanted Englishmen along the coast and less than 80,000 Frenchmen in all the vastness of Canada.

From their numbers the English should have had no difficulty in overwhelming the French and driving them out at any time. The trouble was that the numbers

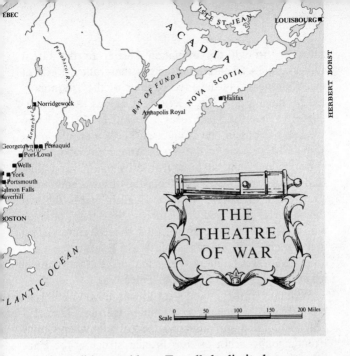

THE
THEATRE
OF WAR

HERBERT BORST

somehow did not add up. For all the limited manpower
of the French colony, it was unified under one government directly responsible to the king. The English had
thirteen separate colonies, settled by various colonists
at various times for various reasons. The idea of united
action simply did not occur to them. Indian raids in
New York's Mohawk Valley did not trouble the sleep
of Virginians; farmers in New Jersey were not concerned with scalpings along the Massachusetts borders.
It took the drawn-out French and Indian Wars just to
begin to bring the colonies together.

From the start the French formed a trading alliance
with the Algonquin and Huron tribes to the west. Before long the formidable Iroquois of the Mohawk Valley began—in modern terms—to hijack the fur-laden
canoes of the Hurons. The Mohawk Valley was the one

13

gateway through the mountain barrier to the Great Lakes and to Canada, and across that valley, lords of the wilderness, lay the Five Nations of the Iroquois— the Mohawks, Senecas, Cayugas, Oneidas, and Onondagas. (When the Tuscaroras joined in 1713, it became the Six Nations of the Iroquois.) These were the most able and ferocious of the North American tribes, fearing no others, and in turn, feared by all. At first they traded with the Dutch, then later they traded and tentatively allied themselves with the English, and in the end they nearly destroyed the Hurons. But their alliance was always an uncertain one, and they became skilled in balancing the French against the English for their own advantage. Such was the situation in North America at the beginning of King William's War.

William III of England went to war in May, 1689, to block France's attempt to dominate Europe. The next year the conflict spread across the Atlantic when Count Frontenac, governor of New France, struck at the English colonies.

The indomitable Frontenac, although now seventy years old, had been sent to Quebec by his king the previous autumn as governor for the second time. It was high time that such a man of action should arrive, for the heart had gone out of the despairing little colony. The Iroquois had grown contemptuously bold in their attacks. Not long before Frontenac's arrival, a large band overwhelmed the settlement of Lachine, near Montreal, slaughtering 200 men, women, and children and taking 120 captives; within sight of Montreal they put their prisoners to the torture fires. The tribes of the Great Lakes were writing off their French allies and making overtures to the Five Nations. It was Frontenac's task to revive the failing colony, set the Iroquois by the heels, and restore French prestige by dealing a

14

smashing blow at the English.

The result was the Schenectady massacre. Frontenac's raiding party was commanded by Nicholas de Mantet. With him went 140 Indians and 160 of the hardy woodsmen-fighters called *coureurs de bois*—runners of the forest. Their original goal had been Albany, the key trading center for the Iroquois. The winter march from Montreal was so terrible, however, that Mantet's party chose the smaller and weaker village of Schenectady.

Some six weeks later Frontenac's men struck again, this time in New England. A band of French and Indians under François Hertel made a sudden terror raid on Salmon Falls at the boundary of New Hampshire and the northern part of Massachusetts that later became Maine. Like Schenectady, Salmon Falls dozed in false security under its blanket of snow. No sentries manned its two small forts. Just before the stars began to fade, Hertel's men surrounded the settlement. As a cold March dawn flickered in the east, they attacked.

The dazed settlers were hauled from their beds and shot or tomahawked on the spot. There was almost no resistance. Thirty were killed. Fifty-four others, mostly women and children, were made prisoners, the cattle were slaughtered, and the torch put to the settlement. When the French learned that the alarm had been raised in Portsmouth and a large avenging force was on the way, they slipped off with their wailing prisoners, leaving behind them smoldering wreckage and red-stained snow. At sunset the outnumbered French column turned to face the pursuers at a narrow bridge over the Wooster River. Through the long-shadowed twilight Hertel and his men fired from the far end of the bridge, picking off the too-eager English until it was dark enough to slip away.

But even with his mission safely accomplished, Hertel was still not ready to return to Canada. In May, 1690, he joined Frontenac's third attacking column, which was under the leadership of a young French nobleman named Portneuf and included several hundred Abenaki Indians eager for scalps and plunder. An attack was planned on Fort Loyal at Casco Bay.

Fort Loyal was a scanty, palisaded settlement on the site of what is now Portland, Maine. Its garrison was small and, like the others, unsuspecting. Portneuf and Hertel might have taken it by surprise if the Abenaki had not spotted a Scotsman about a mile from the fort. His red hair was too much of a temptation, and with a whoop, they were on him. The echoing scalping cries roused the garrison commanded by Captain Sylvanus Davis. Maddened by the sound, a brave and foolish

ONONDAGA HISTORICAL ASSOCIATION

Leading a raid against the Iroquois in 1696, New France's governor, Count Frontenac (seated at the far right), watches his Indian allies torture a captive.

young lieutenant, Thaddeus Clark, led out thirty volunteers. With a cheer his men raced forward—into a waiting trap. The luckier volunteers died at the first volley; the rest were hacked to death and scalped.

As soon as he saw the swarming numbers of the attackers, Davis realized that defense could be only temporary. He asked the French for terms—terms which were granted all too easily. The garrison was offered safe-conduct to the next town. Davis' experience should have made him realize that against the blood-lusting Abenaki a French promise of safety would mean little, even if French intentions were honorable. And so it turned out: as the men, women, and children emerged through the sagging gates, they were seized by the Indians and either scalped on the spot or dragged off as captives. Only Davis and a few others

remained alive to be taken finally to Quebec.

These cruel episodes gave heart to the disheartened French, restoring in blood the courage of their dreams. No longer did the lake Indians look south to the Iroquois. In turn the English colonies saw war range across the horizon like a threatening thunderhead from which lightning might strike at any point.

Massachusetts was first to launch a successful counterattack against the French. The Bay Colony's commerce suffered much from the raids of French cruisers harboring at Port Royal in Acadia (now Nova Scotia). An expedition was sent out from Boston in April under Sir William Phips to destroy this osprey's nest. It consisted of seven ships with 280 sailors and nearly 500 militiamen, and the thirty-nine-year-old Sir William was just the man to lead it.

He was born Lucky Billy, his mother's twenty-first child—which, as seven times three, is lucky in itself. A farm boy from the bloody border region, Phips learned the trade of ship's carpenter, and at the age of thirty came to Boston with nothing more than a pair of brawny shoulders, a rough, persuasive tongue, and his tradesman's skill. Soon he married a prosperous widow who, it is said, taught him to read and to write. Now, Billy became William the shipbuilder and later a captain in the West Indies trade, where he picked up gossip of the sunken treasure fleets of Spain. He managed to persuade King Charles II of England to back an expedition that, in 1687, located a treasure galleon that had gone to the bottom sixty years before. He recovered thirty-three tons of coin and bullion, enough to make his backers and himself rich. A grateful king, now James II, made him Sir William, the first American to become a knight.

Sir William's luck still held when his ships with their

seasick militiamen sailed challengingly into Port Royal harbor in May, 1690. A ramshackle fort held a garrison of only seventy, and the timid Governor Meneval surrendered at once. Phips sent patrols to reduce the other stations along the coast, and all Acadia fell like a ripe apple. So Lucky Billy returned triumphantly to Boston with no casualties and much loot.

He found Boston as angry as a kicked hornet's nest over the news of the French-Indian attacks on the border settlements. If Frontenac had thought his quick, brutal raids would make the English cringe back into their coastal towns, he did not know his enemies. New Yorkers were getting together a land expedition against Montreal, and the citizens of Massachusetts decided to equip a squadron to take Quebec. And who could be better suited to take command than Sir William Phips? "I am the best man in Boston to handle it," he modestly agreed when he was approached. No matter that the state treasury was empty; funds could be borrowed against Sir William's return with the plunder of Quebec.

Sir William, general and admiral, sailed on August 9, 1690, with three ships of war and twenty-nine trading and fishing vessels of assorted sizes, to be joined under way by three more ships sent from New York. All in all, he commanded 1,300 militiamen and 900 sailors and auxiliaries. Seas and winds kept contrary, and the St. Lawrence proved to be a tricky river to navigate. Not until late September did the Massachusetts flotilla anchor at Tadoussac, 125 miles from Quebec. Lucky Billy's luck, however, was still with him, for the French were unaware of his threat to the heart of New France.

Yet instead of thrusting ahead with his old devil-may-care confidence, Phips anchored off Tadoussac for three weeks, holding councils of war, talking and planning, while all the time his precious luck was slipping

19

between his unclenched fingers.

Frontenac had left Quebec to see about the rumored threat to Montreal from the New York expedition, and there were only two hundred soldiers in the citadel. Major Prévost had done his brave best to strengthen the fortifications and set up cannon, but nothing could have saved him if Phips's squadron had suddenly appeared before the city. Why Lucky Billy missed his biggest chance will never be known, but miss it he did.

As soon as Prévost learned of the hostile fleet at Tadoussac, he rushed word to Frontenac. The poorly planned New York effort had collapsed, and Frontenac was free to return with all speed by canoe. He left word that every available man was to be sent after him, and he arrived with three hundred of his soldiers just the day before the English sails finally appeared in the basin below Quebec's towering rock.

Sir William might pass muster as an admiral, but as a general he was an amateur. His first gesture was a ridiculous demand for Quebec's surrender, which Frontenac dismissed with haughty contempt. Even as Phips patched together a plan of attack, shrilling fifes and the beat of drums from the heights announced the arrival of French reinforcements. "My faith," a French prisoner told Phips, "you have lost the game!"

Phips's plan was to land 1,300 militiamen led by Major John Walley downriver from Quebec, cross the St. Charles River, gain the high ground beyond it, and storm the town from the rear. Meanwhile, Sir William would take his fleet directly below the stone fortifications and blast the heights.

October had begun to sprinkle the land with frost. Sickness crept through the New England army, already discouraged by a deserter's report that there were now 3,000 French within Quebec. Nevertheless, Walley and

20

In this portrait Sir William Phips wears the proud and confident expression of the conqueror of Acadia rather than the look of a man who was to taste defeat at the gates of Quebec.

COLLECTION OF
MRS. WILLIAM TUDOR GARDINER

his men waded ashore according to plan, crawling through freezing muck to establish their position. For three days they held their beachhead, while ice formed an inch thick in the puddles, smallpox spread, and food failed. When Sir William tried to bombard the citadel, he made the unhappy discovery that it is easier to shoot down than up. His cannonading did no great harm, but French counterfire raked the fleet and put his flagship out of action. Powder was running short, the ships were leaking, and there was nothing to do but weigh anchor and let the crippled flotilla drift out of range. Walley's men were brought off as Phips watched sadly, knowing his grand campaign was over.

He had just enough luck left to get most of his expedition home. Nevertheless, the New Englander's instinct was true. Quebec was the heart of Canada, as could be said of no one city in the English colonies. And even though the English gauntlet had been thrown down in bungling failure, it had been thrown in a gesture that would not be forgotten. As the colonists would gradually realize, here was the beginning of an enormous game of destiny.

2.

The Conflict Widens

PHIPS AND HIS BATTERED FLOTILLA had sailed away, but in Quebec one enemy still lurked behind—famine. New France did not grow enough food to support itself, and English ships now blockaded the mouth of the St. Lawrence River. Only one French supply ship in three was lucky enough to slip past to Quebec. The Iroquois seemed able to scent weakness and stepped up their hit-and-run raids. Frontenac had to use soldiers to guard the men working in the fields.

The stern old governor decided that the Iroquois needed a lesson that neither they nor the other tribes would forget. Again he sent out Nicholas de Mantet with one hundred hand-picked soldiers and several hundred militiamen and Christian Indians—Iroquois who had been converted by Jesuit missionaries and lived in a village near Montreal.

It was another of those bitter winter expeditions. Mantet, who left Chambly in January, 1693, managed to reach the Mohawk Valley and destroy three Mohawk towns, taking three hundred captives. His Christian Indians, however, moved reluctantly against their cousins. Mantet was finally forced back by Peter Schuyler, the mayor of Albany and a brave and aggressive field commander. Mantet's men almost starved before they reached Quebec, being reduced to eating bark, scratching for roots, and even stewing their moccasins. The frozen scarecrows who tottered through the Quebec gate looked and felt little like conquering heroes. Nevertheless, Frontenac was well satisfied. The Mohawks realized that he was not a man to fool with, and the wavering western tribes began once again to send their furs to Montreal and Quebec.

Following Phips's capture of Port Royal and all of

Count Frontenac is shown in this heroic statue as he appeared at the height of his long career as governor of New France.

Louis XIV, shown in the magnificent Gobelin tapestry above, was king of France from 1643 to 1715.

For much of his fourteen-year reign, England's William III, seen at the right, fought the France of Louis XIV.

Acadia in 1690, its reluctant inhabitants swore an oath of allegiance to the English sovereigns, William and Mary. But Lucky Billy left behind no garrison when he sailed back to Boston; as far as the Acadians were concerned, he took their oath with him. Acadia, then made up of Nova Scotia, New Brunswick, and northern Maine, was a no man's land between New France and New England. Whoever held the region needed the support and allegiance of the Abenaki. And Indian support was apt to prove here in the morning and gone in the afternoon. The only way to control Acadia, Frontenac realized, was to keep the Abenaki hating the English, to stir them up by organizing terror raids against New England.

Frontenac appointed the Chevalier Robineau de Villebon as governor of Acadia, with instructions to "put forth all your ability and prudence to prevent the Abenaki from occupying themselves in anything but war." Villebon proceeded to sow seeds of hate. "Not even infants in the cradle are [to be] spared," he commanded. The French attack was to be carried to New England doorsteps, silently and relentlessly.

Father Thury, a warrior-priest who had developed a great hold over the Abenaki, stirred them into action. He honestly believed the English to be the enemies of God. In the sharp cold of February, 1692, he led a band of 150 Abenaki against the little settlement at York, Maine. It was the same old grisly story—days that seemed too cold for anyone to endure outdoors, a careless garrison, snow obscuring the landscape; then in the middle of the swirling flakes the war whoops of the attackers. Before the settlers could rouse themselves for defense, over half were dead or captured.

When the English had a chance to prepare, however, the Abenaki found their war whoops dying in their throats. At first the pillage of York echoed headily through the wigwams, and more Abenaki came to Father Thury's band. By early summer he had joined with Villebon's brother, Portneuf, for an attack on Wells. Together they gathered over four hundred warriors. But Wells had taken a lesson from nearby York, and this time there was no surprise. There were only thirty armed men of the garrison manning the wooden barricades, but their guns were ready and their aim was good. To take Wells the Abenaki would have to make a direct assault under fire. This was not the kind of fighting they relished. Neither Father Thury's fierce words nor Portneuf's promised gifts could drive them on. The thirty determined men behind the barricades drove them off, and the Abenaki began to have second thoughts about the English.

Meanwhile Sir William Phips, recovered from any discouragement over his Quebec fiasco, had sailed for England. Nor did King William seem to harbor any bad feelings about the lost campaign; in fact, he sent Lucky Billy back as governor of Massachusetts.

Phips's problem was to protect the isolated border settlements of the colony, and to do this he planned a chain of forts. At Pemaquid, not far from his birthplace, he built the first fort, a menacing quadrangle of stone dominating the Kennebec and Sheepscot rivers. To the Abenaki the massive walls, resistant to shot and fire, were a sign that the English meant business. They began to trickle in to talk about peace.

As soon as Frontenac heard about Pemaquid being fortified, he sent Pierre d'Iberville, with two warships, to put a stop to such English insolence. The expedition was unlucky from the beginning and stayed that way. A Quebec captive managed to get advance word to Boston. When d'Iberville picked up the false rumor that a fleet was being readied in Boston for another thrust against Quebec, he turned back without even making an assault.

Not for three years did Frontenac make a second attempt. In 1696 he again sent d'Iberville and the warships, but this time the expedition was stiffened by the presence of the Baron de St. Castin and Father Thury, with his Indian auxiliaries. At Pemaquid the garrison of ninety-five militiamen was commanded by one Pascho Chubb, a man known to history only for his brief and cowardly defense. The French landing party invested the fort and lobbed four or five bombshells over the granite walls; Chubb issued some heroic bluster and at once surrendered on the promise of safe-conduct—a promise which for once the French kept. D'Iberville's men then leveled the walls of Phips's pride.

As an advance base Pemaquid was a threat to all Acadia. With its fall Boston lost its shield and lay open to any French sea-borne attack. If Quebec was the heart of New France, Boston with its 7,000 inhabitants was the heart of New England. The wily Frontenac could read a map like a book and had grasped that fact long ago. Pemaquid's destruction gave him his big chance. He knew many Bostonians were fishermen who would be away at sea. At the most, the city could count on some eight hundred defenders.

Frontenac planned to set out from Quebec with 1,600 attackers. He was to be joined by fifteen French warships under the Marquis de Nesmond, forming an overwhelming force that Boston would have no chance of resisting. Once the Puritan town had been taken and destroyed, the French could move up the coast to deal with Salem and Portsmouth. Such a stroke would be the beginning of the end for the English colonies and the English empire in North America. So Frontenac saw the plan develop in his mind's eye.

During the spring and summer of 1697 he made his preparations; transports lay ready in the basin of Quebec, the soldiers impatient for Nesmond's squadron. The maples were beginning to turn, and still not a sail had appeared. Finally, a ship arrived with the news that Nesmond had been detained by contrary winds, that the stalled fleet had only fifty days' provisions left, and that it was too late this year for such an attack. Frontenac realized bitterly that now it was too late in any year for him. The seventy-seven-year-old governor doubted that in his lifetime the English colonies would again be so ripe for the taking. He was right, for within a year he was dead.

Meanwhile French-Indian war parties struck from the Kennebec to the Connecticut with increasing cruelty. Scores of scalped corpses lay among the smoking ruins of tiny settlements. The heartsick, bodysick captives trudged despondently along the forest trails to Canada, prodded and taunted by their painted captors. Anyone—man, woman, or child—who could not keep up was cut down by a tomahawk. Seldom could the captives pay the Indians back in kind for such treatment. Haverhill's Hannah Dustin, though, was one of those who could and did.

Haverhill lay thirty miles north of Boston, a frontier settlement like York or Wells, with outlying farms and a fortified blockhouse to which settlers could make a quick retreat when the drum beat a warning. There were rumors of Indians in the vicinity one raw March morning in 1697, but Colonel Nathaniel Saltonstall, responsible for the public safety, gave no warning order.

No one observed the silent enemy shapes slipping in and out of the leafless thickets, following the trail to Haverhill. These were Abenaki from the French mission on the Chaudière River, and they were more a hunting than a war party, for they had brought squaws and children with them. A few briskly determined rounds from the blockhouse would certainly have held them off. But the village was completely unprepared. It was the kind of attack the Indians always aimed for: surprise too complete for resistance; quick murder, pillage, and flame; and then off silently with their captives through the protecting woods. Thus was a large part of Haverhill destroyed; twenty-seven inhabitants, mostly women and children, were killed, and thirteen prisoners were carried away.

Among the prisoners was Hannah Dustin, who lived on one of the outlying farms. At the time of the attack, her husband, Thomas, was in the fields with seven of their children, aged two to seventeen. He had left his wife and their week-old baby behind in the care of a neighbor, Mary Neff. When the Indians smashed their way in, Hannah was upstairs in bed with the baby. One of the braves seized her and dragged her downstairs. Another snatched up the baby and killed it in front of her. She and Mary Neff were hustled north with the other captives while Haverhill crackled in flames.

Thomas Dustin was too late to save his wife and infant and his flaming house, but he managed to place himself with his musket between the savages and his seven children, holding off the attackers with well-placed shots until the children were able to reach the blockhouse, a mile away.

No one attempted to follow the Indians. Soon they split up into small bands and divided their captives. Hannah and Mary and a young boy, Samuel Lenorson, who had been taken prisoner in an earlier raid, were given over to a band consisting of four warriors, a squaw, and six children. The warrior whose slave and servant Hannah now became spoke English. He had lived with an English family in Lancaster, Massachusetts, where he had learned the language and enjoyed the Puritan prayers, although now he preferred French-taught Catholicism.

The death of Hannah's baby must have turned her heart to steel and given her a strength beyond despair. She lived only for revenge. Sometimes the Indians would taunt the white women, promising them that when they reached the Abenaki village, they would be stripped and forced to run the gantlet before being sold to the French. Each night the Abenaki slept snugly around the campfire, leaving their captives on the outer edge of cold. There was no fear of their escaping, for without food, in a wilderness, there was no place they could go.

A month and a half later, when the band had gone about half their journey, they camped for the night on a small island in the Merrimack River. Hannah had long since formed her plan, and now she explained it to Mary and the boy, Samuel. Late that night, as the Indians lay around the fading fire in deepest sleep, the three whites crept toward them. Hannah had stolen a hatchet, and now the other two picked up tomahawks. They waited, each poised over a victim, and as Hannah gave the signal all three struck. With quick, desperate accuracy they split the skulls of the four warriors and then turned on the squaw and children.

The whites picked their way among the corpses, searching for food in the Indian stores. This they packed carefully and took an Indian musket as well. As the morning light filtered across the water, they were ready to start off down the river. But just before they left, Hannah picked up a knife, bent over the bodies, and lifted their scalps. With these bloody tokens of revenge she and her companions made their way back to Haverhill.

Hannah Dustin is only one example of the new hardness with which the English settlers were reacting to the French-Indian challenge. Savagery bred savagery. In the latter part of the long conflict Rogers' Rangers could rival any Indian band in ambush, murder, and scalpings.

Such savagery became a legend in the person of Tom Quick. This broad-shouldered, bearded, high-cheekboned hunter with cold gray eyes and a hawk nose grew to be the most noted Indian killer between the Blue Ridge Mountains and the Catskills. He became first known as a hunter of red men in the French and Indian Wars and lived on until after the American Revolution. From boyhood to old age his one passion was killing Indians. His deadly seven-foot four-inch musket, Long Tom, was better known than many a real person in the Delaware Valley. For Quick, as for the Indians, the best way of killing was the easiest—a shot in the back. Once, after Tom waylaid an Indian and squaw with two young children and killed them all, he was asked why he had not spared the children. "Because," he answered, "nits make lice."

Tom Quick, one of five children, was born in 1734 in a cabin in Milford, Pennsylvania, on the upper Delaware close to the borders of New York and New Jersey. Brought up on the frontier, he was familiar with Indians from the time he could crawl. Those taciturn braves were at first friendly, moving in and out of the Quick house at will, bringing the white children gifts of feathers and plumes and furs. Tom played with their children, spoke their guttural tongue as well as he spoke English, ate their food, and learned their forest ways. It was the life he loved. But as Tom grew older, more settlers encroached on the tribal hunting grounds, and the Indians' friendship cooled.

One winter when he was twenty-two and was crossing the frozen river with his brothers and his father, they were ambushed by a band of Delawares on the bank. Tom's father dropped mortally wounded, and Tom himself was nicked by a bullet. As the Indians swept down on them, the father ordered his sons to leave him—their only hope of escape. When the boys reached safety Tom looked back, and far off across the flat gray ice he saw the Indians clustered round the sprawled, motionless figure. Then the war whoop echoed, and the knives flashed briefly as they took the old man's scalp. Watching in agony, Tom Quick swore then that he would avenge his father by killing a hundred Indians, no matter how.

Year after year the stories grew round him and Long Tom, as he notched up his total of dead savages. Little he cared whether the English and the French had

In this engraving, Thomas Dustin helps seven of his children escape from the Indians who have already killed his youngest child and captured his wife Hannah.

signed another treaty. An Indian was still an Indian. It was after the peace that he finally shot down Muskwink, the Delaware who had killed his father.

Tom Quick came to personify the vengefulness of the whites to the Indian challenge. He could push an unsuspecting Indian off a cliff, shoot a red hunting companion in the back, murder the trusting brave who lay down at his campfire, and go on his way as untroubled as though he had just killed a squirrel. Frontenac had thought to terrorize the English settlements into submissive retreat. Instead he brought forth men like Tom Quick.

Quick died at the age of sixty-two, only five miles from where he was born. When he was dying, according to one story, he had killed only ninety-nine Indians. To a clergyman who came to offer him comfort, the old hunter begged, "for humanity's sake," that the pastor entice an Indian from down the road near enough so that Quick could use Long Tom for one last shot.

3.

Queen Anne's War

ACROSS THE OCEAN the English and the French were weary of the struggle, and their kings had grown dismayed at the emptiness of the royal treasuries. The peace signed at Ryswick in Holland in 1697 ended the War of the Grand Alliance (King William's War). Few basic issues were settled in either the Old World or the New. Acadia was returned to France, Newfoundland to England, and Louis XIV finally recognized William III as the English king. He might have saved himself the trouble, for William died soon afterward, to be succeeded by his sister-in-law Anne.

When the childless king of Spain died in 1700, Louis found this a long-awaited opportunity to unite the kingdoms of France and Spain by putting his grandson, the Duke of Anjou, on the Spanish throne. Against this power threat England joined with Holland and the province of Savoy to declare war in 1701. So followed the War of the Spanish Succession. In 1703 the struggle spread to North America, where it was called Queen Anne's War. It was limited to New England, with Massachusetts bearing the brunt of it for ten dismal years.

At the time of the Peace of Ryswick, the northern New England frontier was desolate. Then, slowly, the settlers trickled back. The ordinary Frenchman and the ordinary Englishman and even the Indians had had enough of fighting. They had no intention of breaking the peace, whatever the news from Europe. But the Marquis de Vaudreuil, the aggressive soldier who had become governor of New France, was not inclined to peace. Left to themselves, the New Englanders would continue to move their settlements north; left to them-

This view of the Deerfield massacre is from Pastor Williams' book The Redeemed Captive Returning to Zion, *an account of his adventures during and after the raid.*

selves, the Indians would prefer the cheaper and better English goods. "I have sent no war party towards Albany," the new governor wrote, "because we must do nothing that might cause a rupture between us and the Iroquois; but we must keep things astir in the direction of Boston, or else the Abenaki will declare for the English."

Assisted by Father Sebastian Râle, another Jesuit missionary skilled in managing the Abenaki, Vaudreuil set out to scourge the borders and embroil the savages with the English as Frontenac had done. His first attack came on the battered outpost of Wells in August, 1703, to be followed by hit-and-run raids all along the two hundred miles of frontier in the familiar blood-stained pattern of fire, murder, scalping, torture, and devastation.

Among many similar events one suddenly occurred that is like a flash of lightning to reveal all the others. This was the attack on Deerfield, Massachusetts. The very name Deerfield became a legend through the colonies, an omen of the French threat that would never be stilled by treaties, but only by the gun and the sword.

Deerfield looked out over the lush Connecticut Valley, a village of forty-one houses and three hundred inhabitants. Fifteen of the houses were nestled around the wooden meeting house on the rising ground in the center of the village, surrounded by an eight-foot palisade. Since the renewed border raids, the village slept under the protecting arms of twenty volunteer militiamen, and so it slept on the last day of February, 1704.

Deerfield is remembered in part because it succumbed to the largest war party sent out by Vaudreuil. But it has come down in history chiefly because of its minister, the Harvard-educated John Williams, who was taken prisoner in the attack and marched to Canada. Tough in body, sharp of eye, and long of memory, on his return he wrote down all the horror he had seen in a book called *The Redeemed Captive Returning to Zion.*

The attacking force was led by Hertel de Rouville, a son of the François Hertel who had leveled Salmon Falls fourteen years earlier. It consisted of fifty Frenchmen and two hundred Abenaki and Christian Indians. For three hundred wintry miles, from Montreal down the length of New Hampshire, they marched on snowshoes, dragging their sleds of provisions behind them, sometimes through forests, sometimes along wind-whipped, frozen riverbeds. Late in the next-to-last day in February, they reached a pine grove only two miles from the village, and there Rouville halted to wait for the cover of night. They burrowed into the snow to shield themselves from the wind, shivering, grumbling, waiting. It was too dangerous to light a fire, and in any case provisions were exhausted.

While they crouched in the snow, Deerfield slept on untroubled and unguarded. The governor of New York, tipped off by his spies, had sent an unheeded warning. Pastor Williams himself had been uneasy for some time. But in the autumn there had been several Indian alerts, with everyone crowding behind the palisades and all work suspended, and each time it had turned out to be a false alarm. If they kept bothering with rumors, the villagers assured themselves, they would never have time for anything else.

With the darkness the wind blew stronger, swirling the snow in drifts to the top of the palisades, muffling all other sounds. In that time of deepest sleep, two hours before dawn, Rouville gave the signal, and the huddled figures roused themselves, stamped and shook

*Many captives who survived the march to Canada were held
for ransom in Quebec's prison. This drawing is from the jour-
nal of John George, a prisoner there in the 1740's.*

off the snow, then moved ahead. The crust was hard
enough for them to walk without snowshoes.

No one noticed as the advance scouts slipped over
the palisade and unbarred the gate for their comrades.
The only warning was the crash of axes against doors
and the Indians' yelping wolf cry. Like the others, Pastor Williams was in bed when the savages burst the
door open. He sprang up in his nightshirt, grabbed a
pistol, and aimed it at the first paint-streaked face he
saw—in this case a chief's. Fortunately for his life, the
pistol misfired. Instead of killing him, the Indians
bound him and then butchered two of his children before his eyes. In the din a young lodger who lived upstairs managed to sneak out of the window and make
his way half-naked to warn the next settlement.

The bloody scene at the minister's house was re-
peated all over Deerfield. Where men resisted they were

38

killed on the spot, and in many cases the enraged Indians went on to tomahawk women and children. Only at the house of militia sergeant Benoni Stebbins was a party of seven men able to make a stand. The house was lined with brick to make it bulletproof, and the men—old Indian fighters—had enough time to barricade the windows. With plenty of guns and ammunition, they held off a swarm of forty or fifty Indians who, as usual, found they had no great stomach for such direct attacks. Stebbins himself died at the window, gun in hand, but his house survived.

Ensign John Sheldon's house was similarly lined with brick, but it did not hold out after the Indians chopped the door down. During the latter part of the fighting the house was used as a hospital by Rouville. When a badly wounded French officer was carried in moaning for water, one of the prisoners, Mrs. John Catlin, brought him a drink and cared for him as best she could. This she did in spite of having just seen her husband, son, and infant grandson murdered. Out of gratitude Rouville set her free, but she died of grief a few weeks later.

Fifty-three settlers were killed in the Deerfield attack. One hundred and eleven were carried off to Canada, where the Indians knew Governor Vaudreuil would redeem them for gold, and 137 others were able to escape. So death swept like a blizzard through Deerfield as the stars faded, and by sunrise the smoke from the ruined village rose straight up in the cloudless sky. Two of Rouville's men had been killed, two dozen wounded. Within two hours his band with its prisoners was on the trail, and he let it be known that if there was any pursuit, the captives would die.

Whatever pursuit was attempted bogged down in a warm rain that made the country impassable without snowshoes. That night the savages celebrated with rum that they had uncovered in the village, and in their frenzy, killed a prisoner. Next morning it was discovered that another prisoner had managed to escape. Learning this, the angry Rouville informed the rest that if any more ran away, the others would be burned alive.

Williams' wife had borne a child just a few weeks before, and her strength ebbed rapidly as she struggled through the snow. When her husband tried to help her, the Indians drove him off. As the captives came to the Green River and waded knee-deep through the swift icy water, she could go no farther. An Indian killed her with one blow of his axe.

Infants in arms and others who faltered were struck down lest their dragging steps hold back the rest. Seventeen were so killed before the march ended. Yet in some cases individual Indians showed kindness to children, carrying them on sleds or in their arms. Seven-year-old Eunice Williams was carried by a young Caughnawaga brave almost the entire three hundred miles.

At the White River, Rouville broke up his party into small bands which could better hunt on their own while making their way northward. Here Williams was separated from his five children and herded across the jagged, frozen surface of Lake Champlain to the outpost fort at Chambly on the Richelieu River. By this time Williams could hardly crawl along, his feet sliced by ice slivers, his muscles scarcely able to respond to his iron will. The French at Chambly treated him with much kindness. When Vaudreuil heard of the clergyman among the captives, he sent for him at once and recovered two of his children. Eunice, however, was kept by the Caughnawagas. Williams was lodged comfortably in a small parish house just below Quebec. Of the priests there he wrote fairly that they "abhorred

Major Benjamin Church, a veteran of Indian fighting, failed in 1704 to capture Port Royal and drive the French out of Acadia.

their sending down the heathen to commit outrages against the English, saying it is more like committing murders than managing a war."

Not until a year after the raid did emissaries from Deerfield arrive under a flag of truce to arrange for an exchange of prisoners. And not until well over two years were enough exchanges made and enough ransom paid so that Williams and fifty-seven other Deerfield captives could sail away down the broad St. Lawrence and on to Boston.

Some of the children never came back but were kept by overzealous missionaries to be brought up as French. Eunice Williams remained happily in the Caughnawaga village, attended the mission school, and forgot her English catechism. When she grew into a young squaw, she married the brave who had carried her through the snow in his arms. The Indian life became her own. Years later she visited her relatives in Deerfield with her husband, she herself dressed as a squaw and wrapped in a blanket. Her people offered the couple land if they would stay, but Eunice now found New England too strange. She returned to the older, savage life beyond which was only the half-for-

41

gotten dream of her childhood. No one tried to stop her. Three times afterward she visited Deerfield, bringing her dusky children with her, yet always returning to the north country.

The renewed border raids were, as the great American historian Francis Parkman wrote, "a weary detail of the murder of one, two, three or more men, women, or children, waylaid in fields, woods and lonely roads, or surprised in solitary cabins." Again, as in Phips's day, the New Englanders nursed their rising anger. Governor Joseph Dudley urged the men of Massachusetts to attack Quebec, to strike for the heart rather than to try to defend the uncounted border miles.

And in the safe seaside village of Tiverton, Rhode Island, a fat old Indian fighter, Major Benjamin Church, grew so incensed that he mounted his overburdened horse and rode to Boston to explain to the governor his plan of revenge. The major's plan was simplicity itself—destroy the French shield by seizing Acadia. Dudley agreed to allow Church to organize an expedition, which unfortunately was not large enough, nor sturdy enough, nor with experienced enough leaders. Church burned some settlements along the Bay of Fundy, arrived contrary to Dudley's orders before Port Royal with four hundred rustic volunteers to demand the surrender of the town, and when this was refused, could do no more than sail away again.

Three years later, in 1707, Dudley himself organized a larger expedition under the command of Colonel John March of Newbury. For all its size, it had no better luck than had Church. After besieging the fortified walls of Port Royal, March sailed away ignominiously. The colonel could plead that he did not have much material to work with, but Boston knew him forever afterward as "Wooden Sword."

After New England's seven years of phantom border warfare, the first real blow against the French was struck by a tougher and more capable commander, Francis Nicholson. Nicholson, a fatherless English waif, had made his mark in the New World, having been at various times governor in Maryland and Virginia, and lieutenant governor of New York, before he commanded two campaigns against New France.

His first campaign, in 1709, turned out badly. Leading a force of 1,500 provincials and 600 Iroquois against Montreal, he moved up the Hudson River toward Lake Champlain, stopping to await news of the British fleet supposedly moving up the St. Lawrence. Unfortunately, because of the war in Europe, the fleet had been sent to Portugal instead. Nicholson, waiting through the sultry summer, his army falling apart from disease, did not receive the news until autumn.

Undeterred, he and the pugnacious mayor of Albany, Peter Schuyler, sailed for England with four Mohawk chiefs to plead the cause of a new expedition before Queen Anne herself. The Mohawks were the hit of London. Dressed gorgeously, if inaccurately, by an English costumer, they were presented to the queen. The Archbishop of Canterbury gave them each a Bible, the most fashionable artists painted their portraits, and wherever they went they were followed by gaping crowds. After that Queen Anne could scarcely resist the Mohawks' appeal for aid against the French in Canada.

The next year Nicholson determined he would take and keep Port Royal, for whoever possessed that one strong point in Acadia would possess the whole province. The queen had promised him a fleet, but it was not until July, 1710, that five small warships with four hundred British marines sailed into Boston Harbor. With enthusiasm the New Englanders scraped together

1,500 provincials from Massachusetts, New Hampshire, Connecticut, and Rhode Island. September 24 brought the five warships and thirty transports to the narrow entrance of Port Royal's harbor.

Governor Subercase, commanding the French garrison, was in a bad position. He had only 250 soldiers of such dubious spirit that he scarcely dared let them outside the fort for fear they would desert. However, his own spirit lacked only means, and although he could not oppose the English landing, he directed a brisk cannonade against their advancing lines. Nicholson halted his forces about four hundred yards from the fort and began to lay siege in the formal eighteenth-century manner, setting out his trenches while his gunners lobbed shells into the town.

Without impeding Indians, it was still possible to conduct such operations in traditional military fashion. Subercase first sent a plea to Nicholson to receive the ladies of the town, who found the shells distressing. While Nicholson was agreeing to this, the Frenchman decided to request an honorable surrender "to prevent the spilling of both English and French blood." Nicholson graciously allowed the garrison full honors of war, receiving the salute of the French officers as they marched out with their men under arms, drums beating and flags flying. Next morning Nicholson and his officers gave a breakfast for the French ladies. And Port Royal—to remain English now for good—became Annapolis Royal in honor of the queen.

Yet the thought persisted: Acadia was only a province; New France still remained. That was all Francis Nicholson could talk about when he returned to London to see Queen Anne. Now was the time to strike and make North America an English continent. Spurred by the fall of Port Royal, the British government agreed to make this final effort.

The sorry failure of the English expedition that set out in 1712 to conquer Canada has caused it to be nearly forgotten by history. Yet the fleet that anchored outside Boston Harbor in June was the greatest that England had ever sent on a single expedition—fifteen large warships and forty transports carrying seven British regiments. There was a total of 12,000 men, nearly half of them crack European regulars. In addition, Nicholson was to lead 2,300 veteran fighters overland to Montreal. The French seemed doomed.

However, the English expedition had Sir Hovenden Walker as naval commander, about as weak and incompetent an admiral as ever sailed the seas. Even before he left Boston on a sweltering July afternoon, he was beginning to worry about the northern winter. Through a gross error in navigation he mistook the north for the south shore of the St. Lawrence and battered his fleet against a series of rocky shoals. Before he could veer off he lost ten ships and over seven hundred men. More than that, he lost any will he had to fight. The St. Lawrence, he decided, was too dangerous to navigate in any case, so without firing a shot he sailed back to England.

Meanwhile, Nicholson had reached his old camping ground near Lake Champlain where he readied his forces for the advance on Montreal. When the news came at last that the fleet had fled, Nicholson tore off his wig in the blindness of his rage, threw it on the ground, and stamped on it.

In spite of this English fiasco, the weary old French king, Louis XIV, burdened with debts and European defeats, had little choice but to accept the Treaty of

Utrecht in 1713. The treaty's American paragraphs gave Hudson Bay, Newfoundland, and Acadia to England and recognized the Iroquois as subjects of the English Crown. However, the boundary line between Canada and the British colonies remained unsettled. Isle Royale, or Cape Breton, the large island at the entrance to the St. Lawrence, was left to France. Rocky and empty, it seemed scarcely worth owning, but it would soon grow vast in importance to both New France and New England.

This water color shows the fort and harbor of Port Royal, the capital of Acadia, a few years after its capture by the English force under Francis Nicholson. The victors renamed it Annapolis Royal.

4.

The Captives' Trail

VETROMILE, *The Abenakis*, 1866

SOMETIMES, IN THE 1720's and 1730's, French and English ships would hail each other at sea with "What is it—war or peace?" This was a dangerous gesture, for it might be answered rudely with a cannon shot. One never knew the answer in advance. Although the Treaty of Utrecht of 1713 marked off the longest period of peace in the seventy-year struggle, those twenty-five years brought not so much peace as suspended war. A cold war it would be called today, one that very easily turned warm. Then, too, there were local Indian wars quite independent of the French, such as the desperate risings of the Tuscaroras and the Yamassees in the Carolinas to defend their hunting grounds against the push of the white settlers.

The Treaty of Utrecht left many things unsettled. When the French possessed Acadia they had made vast claims for it, but as soon as it was ceded to England, its boundaries shrank to the seacoast area of what became known as Nova Scotia. The no man's land between New France and New England remained undefined; the troublesome Abenaki still glowered in their northern Maine settlements. Did they have a right there? The French said yes; the English said no.

At first the Abenaki, recognizing the surge of English strength, were ready to sue for peace. Eight of the principal Abenaki chiefs from the Norridgewocks, Penobscots, and other bands sat down with Massachusetts' Governor Dudley at Portsmouth and signed their totem marks in allegiance to Queen Anne. If the New Englanders would keep them supplied with presents and trading goods, and keep to their own side of the Ken-

---

The French warrior-priest Father Râle is seen in this print as he meets his death at the hands of New England soldiers. He was killed in an Abenaki village in 1724.

nebec River, the Abenaki would keep the peace.

But the settlers, preceded by an advance guard of sharp traders and land thieves, had no intention of stopping their forward push no matter how many totems were scrawled in Portsmouth. Such indifference to Indian rights and feelings played into the hands of the French and would soon start the border troubles all over again. Governor Vaudreuil wrote: "The English must be prevented from settling on Abenaki lands; and to this end we must let the Indians act for us."

Although Vaudreuil could do nothing directly, indirectly he could do a great deal. He kept the Abenaki supplied with ammunition, and he sent agents who roused them to each new English affront. Those who showed themselves hostile to the English received presents; the others got nothing. Such an agent was the priest-soldier Father Râle, who had lived for years as a leader, doctor, and all-round adviser to the Norridgewock band on the banks of the Kennebec. He lived with them according to their primitive ways; he spoke their language, and he could almost read their minds.

As much as any white man could control the changeable savages, Father Râle controlled his Norridgewocks. Yet even they were hesitant about striking again at the English. Restlessly they watched while the English built forts and blockhouses. There seemed to be too much power behind the English, and Canada was too far away. It was all right to take pot shots at the settlers' cows from a distance or set fire to their hayricks at night, but the Abenaki wanted no full-scale war.

To put a little iron into his reluctant warriors, Father Râle sent north for some morale-building reinforcements. The martial spirit of the newcomers seemed catching, and soon the priest-captain had a band of 250 warriors ready to threaten the settlements. In the autumn of 1721 they besieged Georgetown and burned twenty-six houses. Isolated farms again began to go up in smoke, and isolated settlers were murdered on their way home.

Massachusetts reacted violently to this renewed threat. Râle's scalp was the one they most wanted; to the good Massachusetts Puritans he was the cause of all their troubles, a devil among the Indians. One Colonel Westbrook was sent north with three hundred men, but Râle received warning and hid in the woods while Westbrook bumbled through the village. The furious Norridgewocks now paddled down the Kennebec, seized several small English ships, captured nine families, and burned the village of Brunswick. The governor, outraged in turn, declared war on the Abenaki "traitors and robbers."

Indian raids increased as governor and assembly bickered. Not until three years later could acting Governor Dummer scrape together a second expedition against the Norridgewocks and their devil. Finally, in August, 1724, under Captains Harmon and Moulton, 208 men made their way up the Kennebec. As they approached the village, Harmon split his forces, taking eighty men with him to ambush the Indians from the rear while Moulton made a frontal attack. As Moulton's men peered from the thickets, they saw the ramshackle Norridgewock cabins, scarcely a pistol shot away. The littered village seemed asleep in the quiet warmth of the August afternoon; nothing stirred, not even a dog or a child. Then, as the New Englanders crept toward the clearing, a brave shuffled out of his cabin, saw them, and gave a war whoop alarm as he dashed back for his gun. But it was too late. Moulton let the emerging Indians fire first, wildly inaccurate in their excitement, and then the New Englanders gave them a steady volley. Squaws and children screamed and ran for the river, and the panicking warriors followed. Those who reached their canoes found they had no paddles. Others ran straight on into Harmon's ambush. Twenty-six Abenaki died, as did Sebastian Râle.

There are several versions of Râle's death. The one that is perhaps most characteristic of the man is that at the first shot he realized the English were after him and ran toward them to draw both their fire and their anger and so save his flock. Moulton, however, claimed that Râle kept on fighting from inside his house, and when called on to surrender, said he would neither give quarter nor take it. He was shot down as he was loading his gun. Whichever may be true, he died a brave man, and in his limited way, a selfless one, fulfilling the Biblical prophecy that they who take the sword shall perish by the sword.

To the Indians pity was a form of cowardice. Their captives were no longer persons but things to be exchanged for ransom or tortured for amusement according to their shifting savage moods. The custom of scalping was symbolic of the Indian mind, a mind so apart from that of the whites as to remain incomprehensible. So heedless were the red men of human suffering that the word cruelty seems inadequate to describe their ingenious tortures. Even the gentle Roger Williams called them "wolves with the brains of men."

The history of the English unlucky enough to be made captive did not vary much from person to person: the heart-breaking, body-breaking march through the wilderness; the flash of the tomahawk for those who fell behind; for the rest hardship, torture, and perhaps at the end a slow, fiery death. Some of the captured children who grew up in the wigwams, like Eunice Williams, became, for all purposes, Indians. Others, brought up in Canadian missions, came to consider themselves French, and many a French-Canadian family still bears an English surname inherited from some long-forgotten captive.

The Indians were unpredictable. At one moment a warrior might savagely murder a baby; at another carry an ailing child for weeks along the captives' trail. An Indian might turn gentle, but as with a tame wolf, it was a gentleness never to be trusted.

There is the example of Rebecca Davidson, who was snatched up on the Virginia frontier with her two little girls and a toddling boy. She feared the toddler would be killed. Instead, a good-natured brave carried him in his arms. After a few days on the trail, Rebecca gave birth to another child, and with the strength of such pioneer women, was able to struggle on the next day. Out of kindness the Indians let her keep the baby, but after a few days it grew fretful; one of the braves, angered by its thin crying, tossed it in a river. And after the raiders arrived at their village, the girls who had been carefully tended along the way were killed before Rebecca's eyes.

Some captives survived, either by exchange or by escape, to tell their tales, but there were few among them as gifted with a pen as Deerfield's Pastor Williams, and most of their stories are forgotten epics. One of the more incredible and heroic of the surviving tales is that of twenty-three-year-old Mary Ingles, the wife of William Ingles of the Virginia settlement of Draper's Meadows.

Mary and her sister-in-law, Bettie Draper, were captured by a raiding party of Shawnees in July, 1755. That morning, as Bettie stepped outside her cabin, she saw a band of painted warriors moving toward the settlement. She dashed back inside, snatched up her sleeping infant, and headed out the rear door toward the grain field where her husband and Ingles were working. An Indian saw her and fired, breaking her right arm so that she dropped the baby. As she picked it up, they were upon her. A brave immediately killed the baby. The other braves surged through the remaining cabins. Three of the settlers were killed. Bettie, Mary Ingles—who was expecting a baby almost momentarily—and her two children, four-year-old Thomas and two-year-old George, were made prisoners.

The Indians triumphantly loaded the few horses of the settlement with plundered guns, ammunition, and household articles and set the women and children atop these. They put the torch to what had been Draper's Meadows and headed west, following the course of the New River. On the third night of the journey, Mary gave birth to a daughter. She was strong enough to travel next morning, and the Indians spared Mary and her child and the wounded Bettie because of the expected ransom.

After several more days they reached the Kanawha River, where they stopped at a salt lick. Here the warriors rested, feasting on the game that they shot easily as the animals came to the lick. The women and children were treated with casual consideration. One of the Indians showed Mary how to dress her sister-in-law's arm with a poultice of wild herbs and deer fat. All the prisoners were set to work boiling brine to make salt.

After several days they went on, following the Kanawha Valley to the Ohio River, and continued a hundred miles beside that wide stream to their bark village at the mouth of the Scioto. It had taken them a month to make the journey, and Mary—her baby in her arms—did her best to remember every bend of the river, every junction, every landmark. At the arrival of the triumphant party there was a wild celebration. The warriors divided up the captives. Bettie was sent to the region of Chillicothe. Mary was allowed to keep her baby, but the boys were taken away: Thomas to Detroit, George to some village in the west. She never saw them again.

Escape was perilous. Any captive caught trying it was brought back and slowly and publicly roasted to death. Yet escape was all that Mary thought of. To humor the Indians and still their suspicions, she made herself useful, delighting the braves by stitching shirts for them from bolts of checked material they had exchanged with French traders. Soon she and some other prisoners, including an older woman from Pennsylvania known only as "the Dutch woman," were sent 150 miles farther down the Ohio to the Big Bone Lick to boil more salt.

Besides boiling salt Mary went out daily with the Dutch woman to gather wild grapes, walnuts, and hickory nuts, which they brought back to the Indians. She began to plot her escape. At first the Dutch woman was afraid of such a desperate undertaking, a journey of hundreds of miles through hostile country without food or weapons, with only Mary's memory as a guide. But finally Mary persuaded her.

They each managed to steal a blanket and a tomahawk. But now Mary was faced with the question of what to do with her baby. There was no means of feeding her, no way of stopping her cries that would certainly betray them. Mary knew that if she left her behind, a tomahawk would probably end the baby's life as soon as her flight was discovered. Yet there was no other way. Perhaps some squaw might be kind after all. Late one afternoon she placed the baby in its bark

55

cradle, and she and the Dutch woman started on the long trail back.

Probably assuming that the two white women had been cornered by wolves, the Indians made little effort to search for them. At night Mary and the Dutch woman wrapped themselves in their blankets and burrowed under the leaves. By day they struggled along the faint outlines of Indian trails, wary for any sign of red men, always keeping within sight of the Ohio. Insects tormented them and stones bruised and cut their feet; never were they free of fear and hunger. Whenever they came to a river, they had to follow it upstream to a shallows where they could cross, then retrace their steps on the other side.

By the end of August, nearly two months after their capture, they had gone back as far as the Shawnee town at the mouth of the Scioto. Luck was with Mary Ingles at last, for at sunset she found an isolated empty cabin in the middle of a corn patch. The two women feasted on corn, spent the night in the cabin, and had even better luck next morning when they heard a tinkling sound and found a decrepit horse, with a bell around its neck, wandering beyond the cabin. They loaded the sway-backed creature with corn and started out again. Across the river, lolling in the morning sunshine, the Shawnees were plainly visible, but no sharp Indian eye caught sight of them. They took turns riding and leading the horse, with the comfortable thought that they had something to eat at the end of the day, if only raw corn.

With September the nights began to turn colder, and the cross-streams became more difficult to ford. When they reached the Big Sandy River, about halfway between the Scioto and the Kanawha, they had to plod miles upstream. In trying to cross over a bridge of

56

tangled driftwood, their horse broke through and was lost. The women carried away as much corn as they could and headed back to the mouth of the Big Sandy. Their moccasins had long since worn out, and they tried to protect their feet with strips torn from their blankets and dresses.

The corn lasted only a couple of days, and nuts and berries began to fail them. In their hunger they pulled up small shrubs and chewed the roots. Since the loss of the horse, the Dutch woman's mood had turned ugly, and she threatened to kill Mary, who managed to keep out of her reach while trying to revive her spirits by pointing out how far they had gone.

They had indeed gone far, for through the leaves that had now begun to turn color, Mary at last recognized the mouth of the Kanawha, the river she knew led to home. Elk and buffalo trails made the going easier in the Kanawha Valley, but increased the danger from parties of Indians. For Mary there was the additional danger of the Dutch woman, now increasingly intent on murder. The nights grew colder, the days shorter. At sunset the half-starved, exhausted women crept into hollow logs where they shivered in a numb half-sleep until morning; a few nuts, a few roots—there was no other food—and always the uncounted, forbidding miles lay ahead. They could see plenty of game, but they had no way of catching it.

On and on they plunged into the fading autumn, Mary at last cheered by the sight of the lick where she had first boiled salt on the captive trail in July. The greater part of their journey was now behind them, although the worst—the gorge of the New River—still lay ahead. Somehow the two scarecrow women struggled up that pathless, boulder-strewn, cliff-lined cavity. They walked and crawled through underbrush

57

and thorns, vines and briers, slipping and falling, wading around cliffs when they could, or where the water was too deep, climbing over them. Nights brought frost now and sometimes traces of snow. Somewhere in this waking, walking nightmare the landscape began to level out. There were even soft banks here and there to walk on along the river. But by now the famished Dutch woman had gone quite mad: early one evening she attacked Mary, determined to eat her. If the woman had not been so weak, she might have succeeded, for she was the larger of the two. They grappled for some minutes until Mary managed to break away and hide while the other staggered on in search of her. When the moon came up, Mary discovered an old canoe half full of leaves. With only a stick for a paddle she managed to reach the opposite shore. The next day, continuing along the riverbank, she finally came abreast of the Dutch woman on the other side, who was now full of regrets and begged to be taken across the stream. Mary, however, went on alone, leaving her to howl and wail until she was out of sight and hearing.

It was now, Mary knew, only about thirty miles to Draper's Meadows, but she began to doubt if her legs would hold out. Hunger had exhausted her, and the cold knotted her muscles so that each morning when she woke out of her dazed sleep, it took her some minutes to move at all.

The last section of her journey now loomed up—the New River narrows, where towering cliffs flanked both sides of the stream, and the water was too deep for wading. Near Salt Pond Mountain she came to the precipitous 280-foot cliff known later as Anvil Rock. There was no way around it; she must climb it. As the chill of night came on—it was now late November— she lay down despairingly in the snow, ready to die.

Yet, as the stars flickered and the dawn came and she was still alive, something in the new day gave her courage. This day she would remember as the worst of her journey. Although at sunrise she could not even stand, she gradually forced life and movement back into her legs and then began to climb. All that day she spent crawling from ledge to ledge, clawing at bushes, slipping back, bracing herself against rocks. Finally, at the end of the afternoon, she reached the summit and then slipped and staggered down the other side. There was still light in the sky, and she had forced herself only a short distance beyond Anvil Rock, when she stumbled into a field with sickles lying about and shocks of freshly gathered corn. Help could not be far away. She hallooed and then hallooed again, and suddenly from the other end of the patch Adam Harmon and his two sons appeared, rifles in hand. When they first heard her halloo, they feared an Indian attack, but then Adam recognized Mary's voice. At the sight of them, her famished body, held together for so long by her iron will, gave way, and she collapsed. Harmon and his boys carried her to their cabin. They made her a broth, bathed her, and wrapped her in blankets. After a few days of their care she was strong enough to move on with them to Draper's Meadows.

For nearly one hundred days she had walked, crawled, climbed or waded some five hundred miles through a wilderness that for its greater part no white had ever crossed before. In that time she had not seen a fire and had lived on nothing but nuts, corn, and berries. She had avoided all the dangers—Indians, wild beasts, the mad Dutch woman. And she had survived!

5.

The Fortress

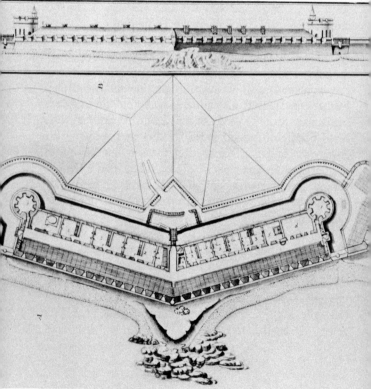

EVERYONE KNEW THAT the uneasy peace between England and France could not last, and each side made preparations after its fashion. The English held Newfoundland to the north of the St. Lawrence and Acadia to the south like two gigantic scissor blades poised to cut the lifeline between New France and the mother country. But in between lay French-held Cape Breton Island, commanding the entrance to that mighty river. Not only would a fortress here guard the approaches to Canada, but it would furnish a necessary base for any French thrust against Acadia or New England. And so the threatening gray ramparts of Louisbourg rose, and New Englanders grew increasingly uneasy.

The new fortress was named in honor of Louis XIV, who was determined to recover Acadia. It was built according to the star-shaped plans of the Marquis de Vauban, the most famous military designer and engineer of the age. The stone walls were ten feet thick and thirty feet high, surrounded by a moat eighty feet wide. There were embrasures for 148 cannon, and it was believed that eight companies of well-trained soldiers could make it invincible. The fortress-town of Louisbourg was built on a spit of land with a jagged granite coastline facing the open Atlantic on one side and a landlocked harbor that could shelter the largest of fleets on the other.

Work was slow in starting, and it continued fitfully for almost twenty-five years. Louis XIV was dead before the actual construction began in 1721. There were troubles with grafting contractors, troubles with shoddy

These are architect's drawings of the Royal Battery at Louisbourg. This battery, the size of a small fort and armed with heavy cannon and mortars, was a key part of Louisbourg's defenses, second in importance only to the great fortress itself.

workmanship and materials, troubles getting settlers to live on that bleak island.

Eventually, by the 1740's, Louisbourg had grown into a garrison town of some 4,000 inhabitants. Yet for all its imposing bulk and its enormous cost there was an important weakness about it: no one was really interested in cultivating or developing the island. The population consisted largely of fishermen, soldiers and their families, and smugglers who preyed on New England shipping. It was a brawling, drinking, gambling town, and—when a day of reckoning came—one without much morale.

In 1739 the peace ended in Europe when England declared a naval war on Spain, known by the ridiculous name of the War of Jenkins' Ear. A certain Captain Robert Jenkins claimed that Spanish customs officials had sliced off his ear, and he roused Englishmen to a fury when he stood before the House of Commons and exhibited his severed ear packed in wool. (It is asserted that at Jenkins' death years later he was discovered to have both ears intact, but by then the damage had been done.) The next year France became embroiled in a war over who should succeed to the throne of Austria; then she went to the aid of her ally Spain, and England too was drawn into the fray. Thus began the third phase of the long conflict between England and France, with war being formally declared in March, 1744. In Europe it was called the War of the Austrian Succession; in North America it became known as King George's War.

Governor Duquesnel of Louisbourg learned of the declaration several days before the news arrived in Boston. Duquesnel was an unpopular and inefficient governor, but this time he acted quickly. He sent a small fleet to occupy Canseau, a fishing center on an island just off the coast of Acadia, fifty miles from Louisbourg. Its surprised garrison of eighty surrendered at once. According to the terms the English would have to spend a year at Louisbourg before being released, but Duquesnel found that he had too many new mouths to feed and shipped his prisoners back to Boston. Before they left, however, they had a chance to look around the great fortress.

Louisbourg lacked enough food and munitions. Its soldiers were mostly Swiss mercenaries, who had not been paid for so long that they sulked by themselves while the governor and his officers bickered. No one seemed to trust anyone else within the star-shaped walls. All this the released English told in Boston.

As if to confirm their story, Duquesnel made a miserable failure of his next sortie, an attempt to capture the Acadian capital. Annapolis Royal's walls were falling down, and its garrison consisted of only about one hundred men. Nevertheless, it was commanded by a man of great energy and courage, Major Paul Mascarene, who held on so tenaciously that after three weeks the French sailed away.

These two attacks alarmed and infuriated the New Englanders. As long as Louisbourg existed, it threatened Boston and all New England. Governor William Shirley of Massachusetts could not get the thought out of his mind that Louisbourg must be destroyed. Finally he hit on an idea as bold as it was simple. If England was too involved in the European war to help out, then the New Englanders would do the job themselves.

William Shirley was a popular governor, with a knack of getting along with such touchy groups as the Massachusetts Assembly. He had come to Boston in 1731, a poor young English lawyer. Able, ambitious, imaginative, and tactful, he found himself governor of

Governor William Shirley of Massachusetts, shown at the left, sat for this portrait in London in 1750. He was in England serving on a royal commission to set a boundary between French Canada and New England. At the right is William Pepperrell, a prosperous New England merchant appointed by Governor Shirley to lead the attack on Louisbourg. Although he had served in the militia, Pepperrell had never been in battle.

the province just ten years later. As Louisbourg began to occupy his thoughts, his restless mind turned more and more to the arts of war. In 1745, as an amateur, he had no idea of the practical difficulties of his marvelous plan. The wise Benjamin Franklin sent a warning when he heard of the madcap scheme. "Fortified towns are hard nuts to crack," he wrote, "and your teeth are not accustomed to it."

At first Shirley kept his plan a tight secret, swearing the members of the Assembly to silence before he would breathe a word of it to them. To the merchants and farmers who made up the Assembly the thought of besieging Louisbourg was not new, but the thought of the colonists doing it on their own was frightening. As the story goes, one of the farmer members was so perplexed that he later prayed in his room for divine guidance—so loudly, in fact, that he was overheard. Soon the news was all over Massachusetts.

After the first shock, more and more people became taken with the idea. To Puritan New England it seemed a crusade against the feared Catholic Church as well as a blow against French power. Overcoming its doubts, the Assembly agreed by one vote. To the more pious it was a sign from God when an assemblyman hurrying to vote "No" broke his leg on the way. Shirley invited the other colonies to join in, but only those in New England—New Hampshire, Rhode Island, and Connecticut—would participate.

Once the project had been agreed upon, a vast innocent enthusiasm spread through the colony. Shirley appointed one of New England's wealthiest merchants as commander of the enterprise, the plump, amiable, middle-aged William Pepperrell. Pepperrell had spent thirty-two years in the Governor's Council and had been a militia colonel. He had never seen a day's fighting in his life, but then neither had any of his officers. At least he was popular with the men, a necessary quality among militia troops who scarcely distinguished between officers and soldiers. Massachusetts raised 3,300 men; Connecticut 516; New Hampshire 454; and Rhode Island decided that the sloop *Tartar* would be contribution enough. It was an eager, comical ragtag of an army that collected near Boston, its confidence matched only by its innocence.

No one had any real conception of what an awesome task it would be for green officers and untrained rustics to storm one of the world's great fortresses. A Bostonian sourly observed that the expedition was planned by a lawyer, had a merchant for a general, and farmers, fishermen, and mechanics for soldiers. Its fleet of thirteen small escort vessels could be blown out of the water by any two good-sized French ships of war. Plans were so detailed that they even included a scheme for making up the lack of heavy cannon by capturing them from the obliging French. Everything was taken into account—everything except the weather, the landing operations on a jagged coastline, the terrain of Louisbourg, and other such practical details.

Governor Shirley began to have a few misgivings and sent an appeal for assistance to Commodore Peter Warren of a Royal Navy squadron in the West Indies. Warren owned much land in the Mohawk Valley and was kindly disposed to the New Englanders. As soon as he received belated permission from London, he sailed at once with three large men-of-war to join them.

On March 24, 1745, the Yankee fleet of some ninety transports, escorted by provincial cruisers, set sail from Boston Harbor in happy ignorance of what lay ahead. Shortly afterward the fleet ran into a northeaster. Snow, rain, and gales sent the ships tossing in the troughs of giant waves and kept the retching militiamen on their bunks in the stink of the dark holds. Most of them soon wished they had never heard the name Louisbourg. Two unpleasant weeks later they entered the harbor of Canseau, which Duquesnel had taken the year before; it promptly became English again. There they remained for three weeks, waiting for the ice to break up in Gabarus Bay on the Atlantic side of Louisbourg. To their joy Commodore Warren now hove in sight with his men-of-war and then sailed on to blockade the fortress.

Louisbourg was expecting the attack. On the mainland, a mile across the harbor from the fortress, stood the Royal Battery—as Shirley had seen, the key to Louisbourg—with thirty heavy cannon ready to join with the Island Battery in the middle of the harbor to destroy any enemy ship that might enter. Forbidding though the stone fortifications might appear, conditions inside them were dismal. The 560 regulars had staged a mutiny, and nobody knew how the 1,400 militiamen might act. Duquesnel had died. His successor was the even more ineffectual Chevalier Duchambon.

Three miles west of Louisbourg, at Gabarus Bay, was a promontory called Flat Point. About two miles farther down the bay the coastline angled into an inlet known as Freshwater Cove. Pepperrell's fleet hove to in Gabarus Bay, and on the last morning in April, 1745, the commander prepared a landing attempt. Several assault boats set out toward Flat Point. Duchambon, guarding the shore there with a mere twenty-four regulars and fifty militiamen, prepared for a fight. But as the boats approached the shore, they suddenly veered away. Before the confused Duchambon realized what was happening, half a dozen English boats were racing toward Freshwater Cove.

It was a close and desperate race, but the New Englanders got there first, plunging waist-deep into the icy surf and up the rocky beach to form a battle line. At least seventeen were ready with their muskets when the defenders charged over the dunes. In that sharp clash six Frenchmen died, six were captured, and the rest fled. The beachhead was established. Before evening 2,000 New Englanders were ashore at the cost of only two wounded. The men sat around their campfires, "singing and rejoicing." As the advance guard lay under the chilly stars listening to the "froggs peep," they had the satisfaction of knowing they had met their first test of war. From rustics they had become soldiers.

The rest landed uneventfully the next morning. Between them and the frowning stone fortress lay marshy

This faded battle flag was carried by the New Englanders at Louisbourg in 1745. Britannia, symbol of England's military and naval power, sits proudly with spear and shield.

flatlands ending in a series of sharp, stony ridges. On the following day Colonel William Vaughan took a detachment of four hundred men to the summit of one of the ridges, where in sight and hearing of the enemy, they gave three lusty jeers. Then Vaughan, scouting through a wooded area behind the Royal Battery's stone bulk, discovered a cluster of storehouses full of tar, pitch, hemp, and sails. These he set on fire, and the prevailing wind spread the heavy, acrid smoke over the Grand Battery like a blanket.

Early next morning, as Vaughan and a scouting party passed the battery, he noticed that the flagstaff was bare. Fearing this might be a trick, he bribed an Indian of his party with a flask of rum to sneak ahead and spy out the fortifications. Creeping through one of the gunports, the brave found the place deserted. Whether alarmed by the approach of the noisy New Englanders or stifled by smoke, the French garrison had panicked and fled.

The jubilant Vaughan and his men at once took possession. So hasty had been the French retreat that they had neither destroyed their ammunition nor completely spiked their cannon. As Vaughan inspected his prize, young William Tufts shinnied up the flagpole and fastened his scarlet coat to the peak in place of a flag. The French replied to this taunt with ineffectual shots from across the bay; then realizing their terrible error, they sent four boatloads of soldiers to recapture the battery. Vaughan's men held them off until Yankee reinforcements arrived and the battery was secured. With a good deal of luck and no casualties, they had captured the key to Louisbourg.

Sloppy soldiers though the New Englanders might be, they had the country boy's knack of making do and fixing things. Major Seth Pomeroy, by trade a gunsmith, showed up with twenty soldier-mechanics to repair the partially spiked cannon. By the next morning he had them drilled out and ready to fire. In their harebrained optimism the New Englanders had brought along quantities of heavy shot to fit the large French cannon they planned to capture. Now this fantastic notion had become for the French a grim fact, for the new Royal Battery gunners soon took aim on Louisbourg.

The capture of the Royal Battery was the first step in putting an iron noose around the fortress. Now the New Englanders began to move their own cannon ashore in flat-bottomed rowing barges. It was grueling work to manage these unwieldy hulks in a running sea, and many were smashed against the rocks. The half-frozen men struggled in the shallows, hauling on cables, fighting against the undertow, and using language that kept the chaplain at a distance. Once the cannon were ashore, Pepperrell was faced with the apparently impossible task of moving them across the swamps and marshlands to the ridge of hills. Hitched to animals, the gun carriages bogged down completely.

Finally another handy Yankee, Colonel Nathaniel Meserve, set the carpenters to work building sixteen-foot-long sledges for the guns. With two hundred volunteers harnessed like oxen to each sledge, the cannon began to inch forward. To avoid enemy shelling, the ragged, barefoot men worked at night, straining through mud and mire, pushing on with furious persistence despite weather and weariness, until in four days they had set up their first battery of six cannon. Each night, or under cover of fog, they brought up more, until five batteries formed a semicircle facing Louisbourg. The last battery to be set up consisted of the guns taken at the Royal Battery. Three hundred men had to be harnessed to bring up each of these. French musket fire was accurate, and many a Yankee died as each night the semicircle moved closer. Frontenac would have made a sortie and perhaps broken up this eager but undisciplined throng with a bayonet attack; Duchambon sat behind his walls in melancholy inaction, leaving the initiative to the enemy.

Gradually the fortress was pounded to rubble by the now-veteran Yankee gunners. At times they overloaded their pieces, double-shotting them, and a number of eager Massachusetts farm boys lay dead beside burst cannon. Nor did Pepperrell's luck always hold. The Island Battery and its garrison, armed with thirty cannon, two mortars, and seven swivels (small guns useful for firing nuts, bolts, chains, and scrap iron at attacking infantry), still barred Commodore Warren's squadron from the inner harbor. To try to capture it Pepperrell sent out three hundred raiders in a surprise night attack.

It was a windy night with a heavy surf when the boats set out, and only with difficulty did they land half their forces. The French remained unsuspecting, and

the assault might have succeeded if the first unruly soldiers ashore had not given three loud cheers. The
French replied with a blaze of gunfire. Some of the
landing boats sank, and the rest pushed off to save
themselves, leaving a band of desperate raiders on the
beach for the French to pick off from behind their
walls. When daylight came, 119 Yankees surrendered.
About seventy had been killed or drowned.

At first the French were jubilant over their solitary
victory, but the jubilation did not last when they
learned soon after that the English fleet had captured
the supply ship *Vigilant,* on its way from France, with
64 guns, 560 men, and great stores of supplies and
munitions. This was the signal of defeat. Louisbourg
and its Island Battery were coming apart at their stone
seams under the blows of 9,000 cannon balls. Powder
was running out. As Pepperrell and Warren prepared a
joint attack, the inhabitants of the ruined town announced to Duchambon that they had had enough. On
June 15, 1745, the French drums beat for a parley, and
the white flag was raised.

Pepperrell allowed the garrison to march out with
honors of war, and he guaranteed the property of the
inhabitants. This was not a popular decision with some
of his New Englanders, who had a craving for a little
booty after the long campaign. "A great Noys and hub-
bub a mongst ye Solders," wrote one of them, "a bout
Ye Plunder; Som Cursing, som a Swarein."

Nevertheless, the New Englanders were overwhelm-
ingly proud of their do-it-yourself victory. They had
proved themselves as good as British regulars, a lesson
they would not forget. They had paid their price, too. A
hundred of them had been killed, and in the next month
a plague would sweep their camp and kill many more.
Fully a quarter of the amateur soldiers who had set out

so blithely the previous March would never see Boston Harbor again.

The news of the victory reached Boston late one night, and the brick seaport woke to the sound of church bells and the echo of cannon. Long before daylight the streets were filled with happy celebrants.

In London the news was received with almost as much joy and with considerably more astonishment. Massachusetts was honored and reimbursed for the cost of the expedition. Warren became a vice-admiral, and

MABEL BRADY GARVAN COLLECTION, YALE UNIVERSITY ART GALLERY

This mid-eighteenth-century English engraving shows Pepperrell's assault troops rowing ashore at Freshwater Cove, near Louisbourg, to establish a beachhead.

Pepperrell became Sir William. Yet when France and England came to sign the Treaty of Aix-la-Chapelle in 1748, Louisbourg—the greatest prize of the war and the pride of New England—was given back to France in exchange for Madras, which the French had captured in their campaign in India. It was a slap in the face of the Yankees, the dawning of the conviction that England's interests were not always New England's, a feeling that the colonists might perhaps be something more than just Englishmen transplanted overseas.

6.

The Ohio Country

THE PEACE SIGNED AT Aix-la-Chapelle in 1748, ending King George's War, lasted only six years, and when war came again, it reversed the old pattern. This time it began in the New World and spread eastward to Europe. With the restoration of Louisbourg the French had preserved their Atlantic lifeline. But now, as English traders and frontiersmen pushed beyond the Alleghenies, they felt their continental lifeline threatened— that vast arc from French Louisiana up the Mississippi and Ohio valleys to the Great Lakes and Canada.

The French were explorers and fur traders who got there first, but the English were settlers who stayed. To the Marquis de la Galissonière, now governor of New France, the one way to keep them out of the Ohio country was to build a protecting line of smaller Louisbourgs from Quebec to New Orleans. In 1749 he sent out an expedition to warn away English traders and to map out such a fortress chain.

In the spring of 1753 the ominous news came to Governor Robert Dinwiddie that the French had built Fort Presq'isle near Lake Erie and Fort Le Boeuf in that part of the Ohio country claimed as part of His Majesty's Colony of Virginia. Dinwiddie determined to dispatch a formal order to the French to leave English territory. In November he sent a tall, grave-faced, twenty-one-year-old Virginia adjutant, George Washington, with a party of seven to carry a warning to the French commander at Fort Le Boeuf, and at the same time, to take a good look at what was going on there. As a guide on that perilous wilderness journey went the frontiersman and fur trader Christopher Gist. Gist knew the wild Allegheny country, understood the In-

---

George Washington was a Virginia militia colonel when C. W. Peale did this portrait in 1772.

dians, could handle compass and canoe, and taught the inexperienced Washington the ways of the forest.

They started on horseback in the last haze of autumn, later took to canoes, and ended afoot in the snow. Washington had never been so far west before. Passing the wedge of land where the Monongahela and the Allegheny rivers join to form the Ohio, he carefully noted that the first party to fortify that triangle would control the strategic river.

At Le Boeuf, where Washington arrived two weeks before Christmas, he was received courteously by the commander, one-eyed Legardeur de St. Pierre. In an informal talk St. Pierre bluntly told Washington that the Ohio country was French, and that from now on, any English who traded or trespassed there would be made prisoners.

Washington could see for himself the preparations that the French were making. He and Gist started back on horses but soon had to abandon their weakened animals and continue on foot. The cold was their enemy now, but they made the return trip in a month—smart time considering the trails and the weather. At Williamsburg, Washington gave Dinwiddie the alarming news that the French were moving into the Ohio country in force.

In the spring of 1754 a band of forty woodsmen under Ensign Edward Ward was sent to build a log fort at the vital junction of the Monongahela and the Allegheny. Ward had scarcely finished his stockade when a French flotilla of three hundred canoes and sixty bateaux rounded the bend. Against this force Ward had no choice but to yield to the French commander, the Sieur de Contrecoeur, in his peremptory order to leave. Contrecoeur now proceeded to build a much larger fort on the site, calling it Fort Duquesne in honor of the

Marquis de Duquesne, who had succeeded Galissonière as governor of New France.

Dinwiddie was fearful that once the French were anchored in the Ohio country they might never be dislodged. Without waiting for word from Ensign Ward, he began to raise a band of three hundred men to reinforce the advance party. Unfortunately, he was faced with an assembly hesitant about voting funds, a public not too interested in what lay beyond the Alleghenies, and a lack of volunteers. Colonel Joshua Fry received command of the expedition, and George Washington, now a lieutenant colonel, was appointed second-in-command. Washington himself managed to scrape up fifty somewhat scruffy recruits.

Early in April, 1754, the young lieutenant colonel, in his trim new blue militia coat, led an advance detachment of 120 men out of Alexandria, Virginia. He planned to use supply wagons as far as Will's Creek, at the foothills of the Alleghenies, and then follow the almost trackless way over the mountains with pack animals. Will's Creek was a hundred miles from their goal. Washington had scarcely arrived there when the dejected Ensign Ward appeared, announcing that his stockade was already surrendered.

This did not discourage Washington, who, when Colonel Fry died, assumed command of the expedition. Even if the forks of the Ohio had become French, he could, he informed Governor Dinwiddie, march to a point on the Monongahela some thirty-five miles south of the French post, build an advance base, and wait for sufficient reinforcements to take Fort Duquesne. His men began to hack a path through the wilderness, sometimes making only two miles a day.

Washington's men finally broke out at an open area called the Great Meadows, where they made camp.

Christopher Gist rode in with the news that a band of Frenchmen had occupied his outlying settlement. Then one evening a message came from a friendly Indian chief, Monacatootha, reporting that he had found footprints of the French only six miles away. At once Washington set out with forty men in the rainy darkness, meeting Monacatootha and a dozen warriors just before daybreak.

Monacatootha's warriors, followed by Washington's men, were soon on the trail like hunting dogs. They found a party of thirty-three Frenchmen bivouacked in a rock-littered ravine only a few miles away. In the damp of the early morning the unsuspecting French were surrounded; then Washington gave the signal for the attack.

It was a sharp and bitter skirmish, and for the French, a hopeless one. Ten of them were killed at almost point-blank range. When the others glimpsed the paint-smeared Indians, they ran in panic toward the English with upraised hands. Washington, under fire for the first time, heard the bullets whistle past him and found the sound "charming." Monacatootha personally killed the French commander, the Sieur de Jumonville. As the gunfire ceased and the powder smoke billowed up in the thin morning sunshine, Washington had his first distasteful close-up of yowling Indians removing the scalps of the dead. He had lost none of his own men, and only two were wounded.

There was not much to the whole engagement—a few score shots, a few minutes' scuffle among the rocks, a few dead bodies sprawled in last year's leaves. Yet in this unnamed ravine the first act of a world war had occurred, not in familiar Flanders or in the fought-over German Palatinate, but in the wilderness of the Ohio country. It was, as the English politician Horace Wal-

The soldiers of the 44th Foot who marched with Braddock wore the elaborate uniform and tricorn hat shown in the 1742 print at the left. Their officers were dressed like the elegant young Captain Robert Orme, seen at the right in a portrait by the famous English artist Sir Joshua Reynolds. Orme, like Braddock a Coldstream Guards officer trained in the most formal British military tradition, was the general's favorite aide.

pole wrote afterward, "a volley fired by a young Virginian in the backwoods of America that set the world on fire."

The French were not slow in answering the challenge. Fourteen hundred men assembled at Fort Duquesne, a force sufficient to overwhelm all the English west of the Alleghenies. Contrecoeur, the commander at Duquesne, sent out Coulon de Villiers, brother of the slain Jumonville, with nine hundred soldiers and Indians to avenge his brother's death. Learning of the French advance, Washington hastily built a rectangular log fort on a low-lying part of the Great Meadows, where his men had already dug entrenchments. He called this makeshift stockade Fort Necessity. It was a poor location, overlooked by higher wooded ground on both sides. At the first real rain, water would flow into it as into a basin.

The young militia colonel had other problems. Of the 384 men on the muster roll at least a hundred were sick. Few supplies were arriving from Virginia. As Villiers approached, Washington's Indians—even Monacatootha—slunk away. To desert when they smelled defeat was only common sense to the red men.

On July 3, 1754, the rain came down in torrents, turning Fort Necessity into a muddy bog. The trenches filled with water. The swivel guns—the principal armament of the little stockade—dripped moisture that rendered them practically useless. Washington could do nothing but wait. At midmorning the French appeared in three advancing columns. Washington formed his troops in line, and for a few moments it looked as if there would be a face-to-face, European-style engagement. But when the French were only sixty yards away they suddenly scattered, taking cover behind stumps and trees and rocks, while the Virginians squatted exposed in their water-filled trenches. From the high ground the French and their Indians now opened fire, picking off the men inside the stockade as easily as those in the trenches outside. The outnumbered English fired back as best they could, but by afternoon the rain had dampened their powder as well as their spirits.

Washington found the bullets less "charming" that day as the brown mud became streaked with blood. The enemy fired at anything that moved—horses, cows, even the camp dogs. By evening Fort Necessity had lost nearly a third of its defenders, all of its livestock, and almost all of its firepower. To make matters worse, a number of the remaining soldiers had broken into the rum stores. There was nothing left but to ask for terms.

It was midnight when the Virginia colonel in his now sodden and soiled tunic signed the surrender terms by the light of a sputtering candle. The French were generous. The English would be free to march away in the morning—July 4—with honors of war: flags flying, drums beating, muskets slung, carrying what equipment they could. For Washington, who had thought of a military career with a royal commission and a scarlet tunic to replace the militia blue, it seemed the end of the road. It also seemed (and for the moment it was) the end of the English west of the Alleghenies. The French had swept the Ohio Valley clean.

France and England would not make their formal declaration of war until May, 1756, but before this they fought a whole year's campaign in the New World. French reinforcements poured into Quebec; Louisbourg, rebuilt, posed a greater threat to New England than ever before. Under this lengthening shadow even the sluggish government in England had to act. The first thought on both sides of the Atlantic was to capture Fort Duquesne. If Virginia militia and volunteers could not manage it, then the task would have to be entrusted to the regulars, those redcoats whose dauntless and disciplined assaults under the great Marlborough had swept the French from Flanders a few years before.

In January, 1755, two regular regiments, the 44th and 48th Foot, were dispatched from Ireland to Virginia to form the core of a new expedition that was to capture Fort Duquesne and give the colonists a lesson in how wars should be fought. The commander of the expedition was short, burly, sixty-year-old General Edward Braddock, who had forty-five years of army service, most of the time with the Coldstream Guards. Smart, assured, considerate of his men, and knowledge-

able in military affairs, Braddock had one fatal lack—
he had no experience in wilderness fighting.

Colonel Sir John St. Clair, appointed quartermaster
general, was sent ahead with an advance party to establish a post at Will's Creek, which would later be called
Fort Cumberland. Colonel Sir Peter Halkett commanded the 44th Foot and Colonel Thomas Dunbar the
48th. Since the regiments were not at full strength, they
were filled up by Virginia companies, whose men were
issued short jackets and known thereafter as "bobtails."
The only colonials who could be induced to enlist were
sorry types who drew Braddock's contempt. The Indians supplied by Dinwiddie were equally incompetent,
and he dismissed all but ten scouts. The rest of the
force was made up of a naval detachment, three companies of Virginia and Maryland rangers, two New
York companies, and a South Carolina unit—in all
about 2,000 men, about half of whom were provincials.

Braddock was tormented by food, supply, and trans-
portation difficulties compounded by a lack of co-op-
eration from the various colonial assemblies. Only
Benjamin Franklin's skilled and tactful intervention
finally furnished enough horses and wagons for the
journey to Fort Cumberland. The Philadelphian was
dismayed about the dismissal of the Indians and
warned the English general against the dangers of ambush. Although inwardly concerned over Dinwiddie's
failure to give him a really effective force of Indians,
Braddock put up a bold front. "These savages may,
indeed, be a formidable enemy to your raw American
militia," he told Franklin, "but upon the King's regular
and disciplined troops, sir, it is impossible they should
make any impression." Washington had written to
Braddock on his arrival, and the general invited the
young colonel to serve as an aide in the campaign.

The trail to Fort Cumberland was bad enough; to the astonishment of the colonials Braddock rode in his coach—standard equipment for an English general. Not until June 10 was Braddock able to push off on the final, tortuous hundred-mile stretch to Fort Duquesne. It soon became obvious that most of the wagons would never make it; the army—as Washington advised Braddock—was held up by too much excess baggage. So slowly did the miles pass that at the pace the English were going snow would arrive at Fort Duquesne before they did. Finally Braddock decided to cut loose, take 1,500 of his best men, with only the most necessary equipment slung on horses, and leave the rest to follow.

Braddock was careful in his advance and alert and meticulous in observing the book regulations. Flankers ranged on each side, and sentinels were always adequate. The French Indians, hovering just beyond the line of march, never dared an attack. The roadbed was twelve feet wide, and the four-column line of march often extended four miles. The historian Francis Parkman described it as "a thin, long parti-colored snake, red, blue and brown, trailing slowly through the depth of leaves, creeping round inaccessible heights, crawling over ridges, moving always in dampness and shadow, by rivulets and waterfalls, crags and chasms, gorges and shaggy steeps." The men soon lost their high spirits. They were tormented by mosquitoes and chiggers; snakes in the swampy areas terrified them, and the shadowed silence seemed ominous.

Fort Duquesne awaited the attack with a garrison of only some eight hundred Frenchmen. An additional eight hundred Indians were encamped in the vicinity, but the news of the vast advancing array was having an upsetting effect on them. Once the English faced the fort with their fieldpieces and brass howitzers the

French would be in no condition to withstand a siege. Braddock expected they might retreat when he arrived. The French, however, had no intention of giving up so easily. As the English neared, the intrepid Captain Hyacinth de Beaujeu led two hundred men out of the fort and tried to get the reluctant Indians to follow. Stripped to the waist in the Indian manner, with only his silver officer's gorget around his neck to show his rank, he finally persuaded an equal number of braves to go with him.

On the evening of July 7, 1755, Braddock reached a bend of the Monongahela River some ten miles from Fort Duquesne. Still there was no sign of the enemy. Next morning the general sent Lieutenant Colonel Thomas Gage across with an advance guard and then Colonel St. Clair with the work details. He led the main body himself. An open way led them downstream to a second ford for a recrossing to the Fort Duquesne side. Braddock made a parade of it. While the drums beat and the fifes shrilled "The Grenadiers March" in the noon sunshine, the ranks swung down the bank into the shallow water. As the lines passed in review—red coats, brass-peaked helmets, blue coats, sailors with rolled-up trousers, artillery teams hauling their twelve-pounders and howitzers, more red coats and regimental standards—the colors kaleidoscoped in the riffling water. Here was the gold and scarlet pageantry of war. Washington said afterward that it was the most thrilling sight of his life.

Gage and his advance guard continued beyond the ford. After a quarter mile the undergrowth thinned and the woods opened up. Suddenly the English heard war whoops and glimpsed the French and their Indians advancing at a run, led by Beaujeu. Gage formed his men into a line of battle across the trail, the first rank kneeling. Beaujeu's band scattered as the English loosed a mass volley, then a second, then a third. The thunder of such concentrated fire staggered the French and the Indians. Their leader sprawled in the leaves, a bullet in his brain. They began to slip away, and for these few moments the outcome hung in the balance. A brisk charge by the redcoats would have sent the French scurrying toward the fort. But Gage's men could see no enemy to charge; unnerved by the Indian whoops they drew back only to become entangled with St. Clair's working party. The French and Indians recovered their courage and their stealth, firing unseen at the confused redcoats. The English fired back, hit nothing, tried to form up as they had been taught, and died.

As Braddock's main force came up the soldiers lost their order. Companies and platoons dissolved. What had been an army became a milling mob, massed together to form a target that could not be missed. Washington asked permission to let the men fight like Indians, but Braddock would still fight in close order, as Marlborough had fought. When his regulars tried to take cover and fire from behind trees, he called them cowards and went for them with the flat of his sword. For four hours the senseless slaughter continued as confusion gave way to panic.

The best of the officers were dead or wounded. Governor Shirley's son Edward, who was Washington's friend and Braddock's secretary, fell with a bullet through the head. Braddock had four horses shot from under him. When he tried to mount a fifth, a bullet pierced his lungs. The drums were beating retreat. Men threw away their guns and ran for the river as the yelling Indians dashed in for scalps and plunder. Washington stayed by his general, placed him in a cart, and saw him taken from the field. The broken and dying commander admitted to his young aide, "Had I been governed by your advice, we never should have come to this."

Although wounded, Gage managed to re-establish some sort of discipline at the river ford, but the retreat was still a rout. Of the 1,459 British troops engaged, 977 were casualties. The others stumbled back along the trail hacked out so painfully a few days before, saved in part when the Indians stopped for plunder. Braddock lived for two days, although he no longer wanted to live. "Who would have thought it?" he kept muttering. At Washington's direction he was buried in the middle of the trail so that the tramping men and

horses and the artillery wheels would obliterate all traces of the grave and keep the Indians from dishonoring his body.

General Braddock, shot through the lungs, is taken from the battlefield in a cart. He was borne along in the backwash of defeat for two days before he died.

7.

Wilderness Warfare

To HIS KING HE WAS Sir William Johnson, but to the Iroquois Indians he was their brother Warraghiyagey— He-Who-Does-Much. This lighthearted, blue-eyed young man, who came from Ireland to America to manage his uncle's estates in the Mohawk Valley, became one of the most important men on the continent and certainly the most beloved by the Iroquois. Had it not been for Johnson, the French might have forged an unbreakable chain from Canada in the north to Louisiana in the south, binding the English to the Atlantic seacoast.

To most English settlers the Indians were forest devils deserving neither pity nor justice. William Johnson saw them as human beings. In 1738 he opened a small trading post on the Mohawk River. There, to the astonishment of both red men and whites, he treated the Indians fairly, paying them the true worth of their furs and selling them quality goods at reasonable prices. What is more, he learned their language, slept in their camps, ate their food, and when in time he was adopted into the Mohawk tribe, painted his face and danced their dances.

He soon became the largest trader in the Mohawk Valley. The Iroquois trusted him and came to love him. He acquired hundreds of thousands of acres—by grant and by purchase, but never by cheating the Indians— and built up a vast domain centered first at Fort Johnson near the river and then at Johnson Hall near today's Johnstown, New York. He married a Mohawk princess, who presided over the Hall as the "brown Lady Johnson." Indians wandered about the grounds

---

Old Hendrick, the most faithful of the Mohawk chiefs to aid Sir William Johnson, poses here beside the tree he notched for each enemy killed or captured.

and in and out of the great house at will. A visitor to Johnson Hall might stumble over them asleep in their blankets in the corridors. "Sir Wm. continually plagued with Indians about him," a young Englishman noted on a visit, "generally from 300 to 900 in number—spoil his garden and keep his house always dirty."

In 1755 King George II gave Johnson complete control of the Indians by appointing him Superintendent of Indian Affairs. No one else had such influence with the red men. Yet it was not all easy. He himself said that he was a slave to the Indians and their demands. When English stupidities and the stinginess of colonial assemblies would have driven the Iroquois to an alliance with the French, it was always Warraghiyagey—speaking their tongue, brandishing the red-painted war hatchet, pledging his own wealth and possessions—who was able to reclaim their loyalty. The English and colonial armies that marched against Canada would have been blind but for Johnson's Indians to serve as eyes. The Iroquois controlled the valley boundary between the French and the English, and Johnson controlled the Iroquois. He was the key.

The year 1755 had been a bad one for the colonies. General Braddock was to have secured the forks of the Ohio; instead, that brave and stubborn general had destroyed his army as well as himself. Massachusetts' Governor William Shirley had the French strong point of Niagara on Lake Ontario as his goal, but he delayed his advance until so late in the year, and his men became so disheartened at the news of Braddock's disaster, that the first autumn storms brought his army to a halt.

Shirley had better luck with a second plan, that of removing the Acadians from Nova Scotia. Although there was a military justification for the removal, the cruelty of it has never been forgotten. For over forty years, ever since King Louis XIV had given them up at the end of Queen Anne's War, the Acadians had lived under English rule. During that time their property, religion, language, and customs remained undisturbed, and they were even exempted from taxes. Yet they continued to look on English rule as something that would pass. Now, as French power revived, the Acadians became a danger. They urged the Indians to attack English settlers, and Shirley feared that they would eagerly support a new French assault from Louisbourg that might well sweep the thin English garrison out of Nova Scotia.

Shirley ordered John Winslow and a regiment of 2,000 Massachusetts volunteers to Acadia. Winslow assembled the hardy, illiterate peasants in their churches, told them they were prisoners of King George II, and eventually shipped them away. He did his best to keep families together, and they were allowed to take their movable possessions. Houses and barns were leveled, and the rich farming country was left empty. About 6,000 Acadians were scattered through the colonies from Massachusetts to Georgia. The largest group finally reached Louisiana, where they eventually managed to create a tropical successor to their lost Acadia. "Evangeline," Henry Wadsworth Longfellow's dramatic poem, immortalized their tragic story, although often with more imagination than accuracy.

One more thrust was aimed at the French that year of 1755. Sir William Johnson was to march against a fort which the French had built at Crown Point on Lake Champlain, threatening all New England. Warraghiyagey had led Indian war parties, but he had never commanded troops before. His Iroquois were upset by French successes, particularly the victory over Braddock, and it took all of Johnson's skill, charm, and understanding to persuade even the Mohawks to take part.

Johnson's opponent was Marshal Ludwig August, Baron Dieskau, a veteran of European campaigns where battles were fought in neat lines and squares by brightly uniformed soldiers. He would have been ashamed to command Johnson's 3,000 New Englanders—farm boys and mechanics and laborers, wearing what clothes they had from home, undisciplined, electing their own officers, soldiers only by grace of the guns they carried. The New Englanders themselves were not sure at first what they thought of their commander. But Johnson had a way with them, and the ordinary soldiers came to admire him almost to a man.

Johnson cautiously led his rough army northward. Leaving some of his troops at Fort Lyman, he reached Lake St. Sacrement, below Lake Champlain, and gave it its present name of Lake George. There, fifty miles below Crown Point, he laid out a temporary camp. A more experienced commander would have shuddered at the site, which had swamps on either side and the lake in the rear barring retreat. But Johnson did not expect the one thing that was going to happen—a land attack.

Baron Dieskau knew all about Johnson's plan from papers found on Braddock's dead, and he prepared to ambush him in the wilderness just as Braddock had been ambushed. A prisoner informed him correctly that Fort Lyman was weakly held but falsely that Johnson's main army was retreating to Albany. Dieskau started out from Crown Point like a wolf after a stray sheep. But though Johnson and his troops were green, he had one advantage. Accompanying the French were the Caughnawagas, cousins of the Iroquois, and Johnson slipped messengers and belts of wampum through to them. Although Dieskau did not know it, the loyalty of his Caughnawagas was shaken. He discovered this when his Indians refused to join a night attack on Fort Lyman.

Finally learning of the French approach the next morning, September 8, Johnson sent an advance party of 1,000 militiamen under Colonel Ephraim Williams and two hundred Mohawks under Old Hendrick, the most faithful of the Mohawk chiefs. Spotting them first, Dieskau hid his troops in the underbrush on either side of the road. Williams and Old Hendrick walked into a trap that snapped with a volley of musketry. The slaughter that followed became known as the Bloody Morning Scout; Colonel Williams was killed, and Old Hendrick fell mortally wounded. The leaderless mob of Mohawks and militiamen bolted for Johnson's camp, swarming across the stumpy field and over the crude log breastwork set up the day before.

Dieskau led his regulars in on the run. If his Caughnawagas had not balked, he could have ended Johnson's army then and there, but the Indians were more interested in collecting scalps. By the time Dieskau could get his forces straightened out, Johnson rallied his men. Crouched behind their log barricade, the militiamen saw the French form up in three formidable lines— white uniforms, peaked helmets, black gaiters, and shining bayonets. They looked invincible. The Caughnawagas, deciding they had done enough for one day, squatted down to watch the fighting.

In slow clockwork motion the three white lines moved toward the English center, one line firing and then dropping back to reload while the next line took its place. The militiamen must have been terrified to see that white tide closing in, but Johnson moved along behind the barrier, cool, jovial, slapping them on the back, until he himself was hit. Dieskau was also wounded as he tried to get the Caughnawagas on their feet.

Still the French came on, although now there were gaps in the white lines, like teeth missing in a comb, and bloodstained figures sprawled among the stumps. Johnson returned to the firing line after his wound was dressed. Dieskau, wounded again, was propped against a tree where he tried to shout orders to his men struggling forward.

After four hours of useless attack the French hesitated and then broke and ran, pursued by whooping Mohawks and jubilant Yankee farmers. Johnson himself saved Dieskau's scalp. Here was victory at last; on the shore of Lake George amateur soldiers under an amateur general had broken an army of regulars and taken the sting from Braddock's defeat.

After the battle Johnson's Mohawks, annoyed at not being allowed to torture prisoners, and feeling that one victory was enough in any case, turned southward. With their going the army lost its eyes. What lay beyond the intervening wilderness, the strength of the French at Crown Point, Johnson had no way of knowing. To fill his need he began to enroll his own white scouts—rangers they were called—from among the tough New Hampshire frontiersmen led by Captain Robert Rogers.

Rogers was only twenty-three years old when he slipped into the pages of history. Six feet tall—a giant in those days—he was hard and fearless, a natural leader whom men automatically obeyed. Anything Indians could do, he could do as well or better. His rangers were forest men, impervious to the weather. On skates they flashed past the French lake forts in the winter silence, and they could fight on foot, on snowshoes, or in canoes. They flocked to Rogers because they found a fierce joy in this life of danger.

European generals believed in settling down for the winter. But even in January blizzards, Rogers led his rangers on hit-and-run raids right up to the walls of Crown Point and ambushed detachments from the half-finished fortress of Carillon—called Ticonderoga by the English. Even the dullest English general soon realized that no army could operate in North America without the protection of ranger companies. In their green and russet uniforms, their hip-length gaiters and fringed skirtlike kilts, the rangers have so captured the imagination of Americans that two centuries later the name was given to the special striking forces of World War II.

Rogers' Rangers had their runs of bad luck as well. Rogers' own hairbreadth escapes were legendary, perhaps none more so than at the Battle on Snowshoes, fought near Lake George in the winter of 1758.

On March 10, with four feet of snow on the ground and Lake George gray and frozen, Rogers and 180 of his rangers left Fort Edward—the old Fort Lyman—to scout around Ticonderoga and, if possible, capture some of its garrison. Traveling on snowshoes, bivouacking in the snow, Rogers could not shake off the feeling of hidden eyes watching him, of some disaster lying ahead. At one point they thought they saw campfires; after dark a squad on ice skates darted up the lake but found nothing.

Although Rogers did not know it, the French had already learned of his movement from a prisoner. As he neared Ticonderoga he left the windswept lake, and at sunrise on March 13, came within two miles of the French lines. Rogers waited until afternoon, when the French scouts would withdraw to the fort.

Rogers divided his rangers between himself and Captain Charles Bulkeley and started up a narrow pass bounded on one side by a frozen stream and on the other by a ridge. He kept to the stream bank, his instinct telling him that if the French came they would advance along the ice. Soon his scouts slipped back to tell him that an enemy party of one hundred, mostly Indians, was moving toward them.

The rangers ducked behind the bank until the French were directly in front; then they blazed away in a volley that killed half the enemy and sent the rest scrambling away. Bulkeley's men ran after them only to find themselves beyond the ridge, facing the main body of six hundred French and Indians. Met by a killing volley, Bulkeley retreated. With superb presence, Rogers rallied his outnumbered force and drove the French back.

It was only momentary. Realizing their advantage, the French counterattacked through the drifts. Rangers and Frenchmen fought hand to hand, their knives flashing, the steam of their breaths mixing in the frigid air. When the Indians began to attack from the rear, Rogers ordered nineteen men to form a rear guard.

From tree to tree, from drift to drift they fought, but the end was inevitable. Surrounded by three hundred Indians the rear guard tried to surrender, but they were tied to trees and hacked to pieces. After three hours the rangers broke, dropping back through the gathering dark, each man for himself. As the French bore down on Rogers he threw away his pack and even his jacket. Near what is today called Rogers' Rock he managed to escape. Some accounts have it that as the Indians cornered him on a hilltop he slid down the steep slope on snowshoes, tied on his skates, and disappeared across the ice. Perhaps the story is no more than a legend, but Rogers would certainly have been capable of such daring.

Through the night, the survivors found their way to Lake George, where Rogers waited. Of his company of 180 only fifty-four reached Fort Edward. The captain, a borrowed blanket wrapped around him, was the last in.

Following Johnson's Lake George victory in September, 1755, an uneasy lull had settled over the wilderness war front for nearly two years. It was shattered in the summer of 1757 when the French took the offensive. Their goal was Oswego, a trading post on Lake Ontario. Oswego was a break in the long line of forts that the French had planned from Quebec to Louisiana and was a potential springboard for an attack on Canada. If New France was to dominate the Great Lakes region, Oswego must fall.

No one understood this better than Louis Joseph, Marquis de Montcalm, who arrived in Canada in the spring of 1756 to succeed Baron Dieskau in command of all the French military forces. Montcalm, whose name would endure above all other French commanders in North America, was a small, dark-eyed, handsome, nervous man whose courage and courtliness were equal to his skill as a general. He quickly began making plans for Oswego's destruction.

Oswego's garrison of 1,000 soldiers and 600 civilians was commanded by the courageous Colonel Hugh Mercer. His men—not the best to begin with—had nearly starved the previous winter and were surly and discontented almost to the point of mutiny. The post consisted of Fort Oswego itself and two smaller stockades nearby, Fort Ontario and the unfinished Fort George. Their wooden walls could never withstand a determined siege.

Montcalm set out from Fort Ticonderoga in July, 1757, with an army of 3,000 French regulars and Canadian militia, a few hundred Indians, and an ample artillery train. So careless was the grumbling English garrison that no alarm was given until Montcalm's men were only a few miles distant. The besiegers fanned out and poured shot into Oswego from their forest cover. Fort Ontario was no match for Montcalm's artillery,

A moment during the Battle on Snowshoes, fought by Robert Rogers and his rangers (foreground) against the French in the winter of 1758, is captured in this painting. The action took place near Ticonderoga.

and Colonel Mercer had to order its abandonment. With it went Oswego's hope; the end was only a matter of time. When the valiant Mercer was cut in two by a cannon shot, the defenders gave up.

Losses on both sides were small, fifty for the English and less than that for the French. But it was a decisive victory, one of the greatest France had achieved in North America. The English captives were marched away. Oswego was burned to the ground, and from then on, New England farmers slept uneasily in their beds, wondering how far this new French wave might go.

They slept even more uneasily a month later. Montcalm, with an army of 6,000 French troops and 2,000 Indians, captured Fort William Henry, which Johnson had built at the foot of Lake George on the site of his victory over Dieskau. The fort's commander, Colonel Monro, was brave enough, but he was outnumbered four to one, his fortifications were too weak to resist Montcalm's heavy siege guns, and smallpox was raging in his camp. After being bombarded for six days, he surrendered under what seemed to be honorable conditions. Montcalm agreed to let the English march out with honors of war, the soldiers merely promising that they would not serve against the French for eighteen months. They were to be taken under guard to Fort Edward, sixteen miles to the south.

Unfortunately for the prisoners, Montcalm was unfamiliar with Indians. The red men swarmed into the fort, heading for the rum stores. Then, maddened by liquor, they burst into the hospital, killing and scalping the sick in their beds. In their frenzy they even dug up the corpses in the cemetery for scalps, planting the seeds of a smallpox epidemic that was to overwhelm the savages. It was grim vengeance for the mutilated dead.

Next morning, as the dejected English marched south along the wooded roadway lined with jeering Abenaki, the Indians suddenly fell on the captives. Men, women, and children were tomahawked before the indifferent eyes of the French guards. Others were stripped of their clothes and possessions; still others were made prisoners for future ransom. When Montcalm heard the whoops and the screams, he dashed up with his senior officers. For over an hour he struggled vainly to control the savages, begging them to "kill me, but spare the English who are under my protection." The remaining English were saved only when a large body of French regulars appeared and drove the Indians back with fixed bayonets. How many were killed has never been exactly determined, but the number must have been several hundred. The massacre of Fort William Henry left a bloody stain on the gallant record of the Marquis de Montcalm.

These prints, published in Germany in 1761, show the uniforms of French troops who served at Ticonderoga during the British attack of 1758. The infantry regiment, represented at the right, fought in Montcalm's front ranks, as did grenadiers like the one pictured at the left.

8.

Grand Strategy

WHEN WILLIAM PITT became England's Prime Minister in June, 1757, his coming was like a clean wind blowing through all the departments and offices of the government. England had lost faith in herself. But now, as Pitt replaced the old familiar, useless faces with new ones, success began to follow the years of failure. He had a vision of England and her American colonies much as Benjamin Franklin then had—a united empire of free people. As a first step to that unity he knew that French Canada must be conquered.

Pitt's grand strategy lay bravely in the year ahead: to launch a massive attack by land and sea. His goals were the three sentinels guarding the gateways to Canada—Louisbourg, blocking the St. Lawrence water route to Quebec; Fort Ticonderoga, on the land route to New France's capital; and Fort Duquesne, key to the Ohio country. For these goals he was willing to strain England's resources by organizing expeditions gigantic for their day.

Against Louisbourg he sent a brilliant but obscure young colonel, Jeffery Amherst, whom he made a major general for the occasion. Amherst's force was made up of 12,000 soldiers and a slightly larger number of sailors commanded by crusty, able Admiral Edward Boscawen—"Old Dreadnaught." The Ticonderoga venture consisted of 15,000 men led by a ponderous, elderly political officer not of Pitt's choosing, Major General James Abercrombie, whom the soldiers called behind his back Mrs. Nabbycromby and the officers nicknamed Aunt Abby. Fort Duquesne was to be the responsibility of the American colonials.

William Pitt, the brilliant creator of England's strategy for breaking French power in North America, was painted shortly after becoming the Earl of Chatham in 1766.

Amherst was one of the ablest English generals ever to command in North America. Yet for all his fame it is easier to imagine him behind a desk than on horseback. In his campaigns he always planned everything, thought of everything, and anticipated everything. Though he could be brave, he was not dashing—and he did not believe in taking risks. So careful was he in his military preparations, willing rather to take a year than take a chance, that he was sometimes called the Cautious Commander.

The French force at Louisbourg consisted of 4,000 soldiers, 2,600 seamen, and a large band of Indians under the sternly vigorous command of the Chevalier de Drucour. But Louisbourg's clifflike approaches, its shield of jagged shoreline and pounding seas, the four hundred cannon lining its walls, made up for any difference in numbers and gave the French a swaggering sense of confidence.

Through turbulent seas and foul weather the English fleet set out from Halifax, Nova Scotia, and hove to just off the Louisbourg coast on June 2, 1757. Six more days of wind and fog followed before a landing attempt could be made. The first assault wave was commanded by Brigadier General James Wolfe, a gallant young bean pole of a soldier, whose dashing temperament matched his red hair rather than his frail body. Soon to be famous, he was then unknown.

While the guns of the fleet blazed a covering fire, two lines of whaleboats set out in a feint toward Louisbourg itself. The real attack, however, was to come from Wolfe's brigade heading for Freshwater Cove in Gabarus Bay, close to where Pepperrell's men had struck the beaches thirteen years before. As the white boats with their scarlet-coated ranks pulled for the shore, the oars dipping and falling in the swelling sea, the land

ahead looked bleak and empty. Wolfe's soldiers had no way of knowing that 1,200 Frenchmen were lying in wait for them behind a barricade of logs.

The French held their fire until the boats were close enough for them to hear the redcoats shouting soldiers' jokes to one another; then at almost point-blank range they opened up a fire that turned the sea to a bloody foam. The soldiers in the splintered boats who were not killed found their water-logged uniforms pulling them down into the sucking tide, and the sailors trying to rescue them were picked off by French sharpshooters. Wolfe had given the signal to turn back, when three of his boats managed to nose into an angle of beach protected by a ledge from the French fire.

Countermanding his order, Wolfe ordered the boats ahead, and as they neared the beach he sprang into the surf, floundering waist-deep among the rocks and seaweed with his men, his Malacca cane tucked under his arm. Other boats smashed against the rocks as they came in, and more redcoats drowned or were shot, but the rest pressed on up the slippery shore, gunpowder wet but bayonets ready. As they stormed up the cliff toward the French breastworks, their fear gave way to the hot, blind anger of battle. Before the bayonets of the sodden redcoats the amazed French gave way and fled to the shelter of the fortress. Luck it was, Wolfe thought afterward, but the landing had been made and the way opened.

After the beachhead was established there was still a month of siege fighting while Amherst developed his plans to strangle the citadel. Wolfe considered his methodical commander much too slow—but fast or slow, Louisbourg's fate was sealed. Daily the English lines crept closer until the heavy siege guns were brought to bear on the granite walls. Fires raged inside the ruined town. The masonry of the ramparts crumbled, and one by one the French cannon were knocked out. There were few supplies and no reinforcements. Drucour had no choice but surrender.

Louisbourg's fall on July 26, 1758, set the bells ringing in old and New England, unused for so long to victory chimes. The captured French flags were taken to London and hung in St. Paul's Cathedral. In America, Philadelphia and New York and other cities celebrated with fireworks and lighted decorations. The delighted Pitt had a special Louisbourg medal struck for his victorious soldiers. "If I can go to Quebeck, I will," Amherst wrote to him. But before he could make plans, there came the news of Abercrombie's campaign against Ticonderoga.

Abercrombie was well named Aunt Abby. He was a weak, fumbling, unimaginative man, who thought in European terms of soldiers marching automatically against fixed points, and he lacked even Braddock's foolish courage. The army that he had been given was more than ample to fulfill its task—seven regiments of redcoats, including a thousand Highlanders from the Black Watch regiment, twelve provincial regiments, and four scouting companies of Rogers' Rangers.

As his army moved up Lake George in the calm of a July morning, it formed a pageant such as the lake had never seen before and would never see again. Rogers' Rangers and the light infantry led the way. There were 900 bateaux, 135 whaleboats, and scores of flatboats carrying artillery, making a line six miles long. The sunshine flashed on the gleaming bayonets; on the scarlet uniforms of the regulars, the blue coats of the colonials, the kilts of the Highlanders, the sober green of the rangers; on the whole great army moving to its doom. The shores echoed back the shrill bugle notes and the drone of bagpipes.

Inside the star-shaped fortress of Ticonderoga, on a neck of land commanding Lake Champlain, were 3,200 troops under the imperturbable Marquis de Montcalm. Montcalm knew that if the English laid siege to Ticonderoga, his supplies would not last two weeks—but he also knew Aunt Abby. Along a ridge half a mile from the fort he threw up a zigzag earthwork across the neck of land, and a hundred feet ahead of this he set a bristling hedge of felled trees and sharpened stakes. He expected that the dull Abercrombie would take this direct route to the fort, and he planned to be ready for him.

On July 6 the English army landed at the upper end of Lake George. Rogers, with a party of rangers that included Abercrombie's second-in-command, the gay and charming thirty-three-year-old Brigadier General Lord Howe, scouted ahead and engaged a French detachment near Trout Brook, a few miles below the fort. The skirmish was brief and the French fell back, but Howe was killed.

George Augustus, Lord Howe, for all that he was a nobleman and a grandson of King George I, was a soldier's soldier. "The best soldier in the British Army," Wolfe had called him, and on his death a provincial carpenter in Abercrombie's expedition wrote, "Lord How was the Idol of the Army . . . he frequently came among the Carpenters, and his maner was So easy and fermiller, that you loost all that constraint or diffidence we feele when addressed by our Superiours, whose manners are forbidding."

Howe's confident presence seemed to assure the soldiers of victory, for he made it his habit to be where they were. To learn the art of forest warfare he had joined Rogers on scouting parties—the only high-ranking officer to do so. English regular officers had a snobbish way of looking down on the bluecoated provincial militia officers, but Howe tried to make the provincials feel they were part of the first team, not just substitutes. He lived as his soldiers did; he ate their common food, slept on the ground, and washed his own clothes. He was that rare thing, a natural leader, and when he pitched forward in the grass by Trout Brook, the spirit went out of the army.

Yet even without this spirit Abercrombie could have won. All that he needed to do was hem in Ticonderoga with his superior forces and wait. Montcalm, without reinforcements and with insufficient provisions, would have been forced back to Crown Point in a few days. And if Aunt Abby had paused long enough to bring up his heavy cannon, he could have cut the French forward line to ribbons.

For a whole day after Howe's death Abercrombie did nothing at all, giving Montcalm enough time to complete the breastwork and the spiked barrier. On July 8 Abercrombie, from his command post a mile

108

and a half in the rear, waited for the torrid sun to reach its zenith and ordered a frontal attack.

The great army advanced to the edge of the rough clearing, preceded by the rangers, the light infantry, and several provincial detachments, who drove in the French outposts and then moved aside to let the sweating regulars advance. Three rows of white-uniformed Frenchmen waited behind their barrier in the ominous noonday heat. Across the field littered with stumps and fallen trees the close-ranked redcoats tried to advance as if they were on parade. Closer they came, their bayonets ready. Then the fire from the invisible enemy struck them, a sheet of flame and smoke. For an hour the English continued to struggle forward, tripping in the tangles of brush, stabbed by the sharpened stakes— brave, easy targets. With trained precision the French followed their drill—fire, drop back, reload, fire. Montcalm, his coat off in the heat, moved up and down the line encouraging his men.

The attack faltered and the desperate survivors began to fall back. Abercrombie ordered new battalions forward. Five times more that afternoon the English charged forward across the fire-swept field over the bodies of their comrades, and each time they were repulsed. In one attack the Highlanders of the Black Watch plunged ahead with such fury, hacking at the branches with their broadswords, that Captain John Campbell and three soldiers actually reached the French lines. As they leaped over the breastwork Campbell was captured and the other three bayoneted. During the afternoon the Black Watch had two-thirds of its men shot down.

By five o'clock the battle was over. The rangers and a few of the provincials kept up a covering fire from the woods so that their comrades could pick up some of the wounded. The English had lost almost 2,000 men; the French less than 400. Abercrombie, his nerve gone, finally ordered a retreat. With an inward mixture of sorrow, anger, and contempt, Rogers covered the retreat with his rangers. But there was no pursuit. Montcalm did not have the strength to follow up his victory.

So far Prime Minister Pitt's grand strategy for 1758 had brought victory at Louisbourg and defeat at Ticonderoga. Now it was the colonials' turn. At the end of

At one o'clock in the morning of July 26, 1758, some 600 English soldiers rowed silently into Louisbourg Harbor and captured two French frigates guarding the fortress. The Bienfaisant, *at the right, was brought off as a prize, but the* Prudent, *hard aground when seized, had to be burned. Louisbourg surrendered the same day.*

August, Colonel John Bradstreet, leading a detachment of 3,000 provincials, skillfully captured the French Fort Frontenac, on Lake Ontario. In one counterstroke the French lost command of the lake.

Then late in the autumn Brigadier General John Forbes, with a force of 5,000 provincials and 1,400 Scots Highlanders, moved on Fort Duquesne at the forks of the Ohio. Forbes was a dying man, directing his campaign from a litter; fortunately he had an able assistant in the Swiss-born Lieutenant Colonel Henry Bouquet. Washington joined the expedition as colonel in command of the Virginia regiment.

Forbes had to face all the usual colonial difficulties of supply, transport, and reinforcements, but he had learned well the lesson of Braddock's defeat. He moved by cautious stages through the wilderness, building blockhouses as he went and dealing carefully with the Indians. Fifty miles from Fort Duquesne, Forbes learned of the desperate situation of the French garrison, deserted by its Indian allies and its supplies exhausted. An advance force found the fort abandoned and destroyed—the ruins of the French dream in the Ohio country.

Abercrombie returned with his dispirited soldiers to the camp at Lake George, where he listlessly awaited the approach of winter. Amherst and five regiments from Louisbourg arrived there in October. What he said to Abercrombie is not recorded, although it can be imagined. Not long afterward, Aunt Abby was recalled to England. During the winter of 1758–59 the methodical Amherst laid his plans for next year's campaign. Again he intended to thrust the daggers of his armies into Canada: from Louisbourg Wolfe would drive on Quebec, while Amherst himself would personally take care of Ticonderoga.

9.
The Great Year

ROYAL ONTARIO MUSEUM

MCCORD MUSEUM, MCGILL UNIVERSITY

THE YEAR 1759 WAS for the English in North America the great year, the year that would see the back of French power broken on the continent. In January, General Amherst issued an appeal to Abercrombie's discouraged veterans—many of whom had simply trudged home after the Ticonderoga disaster—offering to pardon all who rejoined the colors before March. Wolfe would command the Quebec campaign; Brigadier General John Prideaux and Sir William Johnson were to retake Oswego and then attack Fort Niagara, on Lake Ontario. What seemed to all the hardest task, the thrust toward Montreal through the bristling walls of Ticonderoga and Crown Point, Amherst had long ago determined to undertake himself.

By June, Amherst had assembled at Lake George an army of 11,000, half regulars and half provincials. Ticonderoga had become by now such a word of ill luck that the soldiers avoided mentioning the name at all. Some of them maintained that the place was bewitched. Damp weeks followed, with searing summer heat and torrential thunderstorms that swept down from the Adirondack Mountains. The men sulked under Amherst's rigid discipline. There were desertions, and there would have been more but for the Indians lurking in the woods. Finally, in late July, the expedition moved up Lake George, but with none of the bright pageantry of the year before. The water was rough and the wind high, and the soldiers undid their packs and made sails of their blankets.

The men spent the night afloat in "a disagreeable tumbling sea." The next morning they landed at the

---

The Marquis de Montcalm, commander of the French army at Quebec, is shown in the imposing portrait above at the left. James Wolfe is portrayed in the lower picture, a water color made at Quebec in 1759 by a British officer.

upper end of the lake, and Rogers' Rangers scouted ahead. Below the fortress, on the stream connecting Lake George with Lake Champlain, was a partially destroyed bridge; as the fast-moving rangers dashed to the other side they met the first French attack and beat it back easily. The rest of the army followed, while engineers repaired the bridge and Amherst's cannon were dragged up through the darkness.

At sunrise the general led his somewhat uneasy army across the rebuilt bridge, intending to bypass Ticonderoga and set up his siege lines. As he advanced to a rise he had a clear view of the French lines a half mile away, where Abercrombie's men had been slaughtered the year before. As he eyed the grim zigzags through the shredding morning mists he noticed a stir of white uniforms and suddenly realized to his happy astonishment that the French were pulling back.

He spurred his troops forward through gullies and thickets, the men often sinking waist-deep into the mire of unexpected bogs. When they reached the enemy lines, they found them deserted. In the center, as a warning, the French had dug an open grave and set a tall wooden cross above it.

However this sight may have awed the superstitious soldiers, it did not trouble the practical Amherst. He had not been to bed for two nights, but with fresh energy he directed the setting up of siege lines. From the walls of Ticonderoga there came a heavy but inaccurate bombardment.

Within twenty-four hours Amherst had ringed the fort. At the next daybreak the cannon opened up, several well-aimed shots setting fires inside the fort. There were as many French soldiers at Ticonderoga, now under the command of the Chevalier de Bourlamaque, as there had been the summer before. But if Amherst was not an Abercrombie, neither was Bourlamaque a Montcalm. The French commander knew that in a siege he was lost. That same evening he slipped away by boat with 2,500 men for Crown Point, leaving behind a rear guard of four hundred.

Within two days Amherst's clockwork siege tactics brought him almost to the granite walls. He had learned of Bourlamaque's withdrawal; now he observed more boats heading up Lake Champlain from the fort. Three deserters came in to tell him that the rear guard had gone, leaving an empty fort and a lighted fuse leading to the powder magazine. Amherst offered them one hundred guineas—equal to several thousand dollars today—to go back and cut the fuse, but they declined. At eleven that night, July 26, 1759, the fort exploded like a small volcano. For a moment the sky turned orange and the crash echoed from shore to shore; then flames crackled in the ruins.

So the great fortress of Ticonderoga fell. Only sixteen English were killed and fifty-one wounded. Even before Amherst could advance the fifteen miles to Crown Point, that stern fortification was also blown up and abandoned. The southern route to Canada lay open.

If Amherst's task proved unexpectedly easy, Wolfe's task was proving extremely difficult. After a dreary summer had drifted behind the northern lights of autumn it seemed that the expedition besieging Quebec might have to withdraw before winter arrived. The Quebec plateau, dominated by its stone-capped citadel, was protected by six miles of entrenchments commanding the St. Lawrence River, some hundred feet below the sheer cliffs. "Quebec is impregnable," boasted the French governor, the Marquis de Vaudreuil, and so it seemed to Wolfe's frustrated army.

For the assault on Quebec, Pitt promoted Wolfe to major general and gave him a free hand. Even though Amherst held supreme command in North America, Wolfe was on his own to succeed or fail. Failure was something he never considered. In wretched health, moody and distant by nature, with anything but the outward appearance of a great commander, the thirty-two-year-old general with the red hair and the blotched complexion was a born soldier. He had said that he would rather listen to the drum and trumpet than to any softer sound. To him there was no life other than that of the army, and he expected it to be a short one. His consuming ambition was to die heroically in battle, and he seems to have had a premonition that he would not return from the Quebec campaign.

His army of 8,500 left Louisbourg on June 4, 1759. Twenty-two frigates and big ships of the line commanded by Vice-Admiral Charles Saunders led the supply ships up the river without hindrance or difficulty. They arrived twelve days later at the Ile d'Orléans, an island in the middle of the St. Lawrence, in sight of Quebec. Governor Vaudreuil was horrified at the sudden appearance of the British. He had not thought the river navigable by ships of such size, yet there they were in the basin below him, white sails fluttering, decks solid with eager redcoats preparing to disembark. Wolfe's army that now set up camp on the Ile d'Orléans consisted of ten infantry battalions plus special troops —three companies of grenadiers, three companies of Royal Artillery, and six companies of tough American rangers.

June and July passed fretfully. Each day Wolfe watched the tantalizing brown cliffs and the citadel topped by the white flag with the golden lilies. Vaudreuil might be lax and foolish, but Montcalm, in command of the French army, was exact. He knew how to use his natural line of defense. Wherever he thought the British might make a landing attempt he placed guards in prepared entrenchments. He had a hundred cannon mounted along the cliff edge. Although most of his force consisted of Canadian militia drafted unwillingly from their farms, it outnumbered the English nearly two to one. Cautiously confident, he preferred to let Wolfe wither away rather than give battle.

Wolfe's problems were three: the proper place to make an attack; the morale of his army; and the early northern winter that would soon force the British fleet to withdraw. By August half his men were sick, and desertions were becoming common. At first the redcoats suffered much from scouting parties of scalp-eager Indians and Canadian militiamen who fought like Indians, and they had to learn the old lessons that the rangers knew by heart. They were soon camouflaging themselves—turning their scarlet coats inside out and daubing the linings with mud. The queue grease issued for their hair was used to dull the shine of gun barrels. They stuck leaves in their caps, and they learned to scalp. Soon the Indians complained that the English no longer stood still to be shot at.

Wolfe had two strokes of luck, one good and one bad. Across the river from Quebec was a high elbow of land called Point Lévis. A small French outpost there was surprised and captured by a detachment of rangers and light infantry. It was a strategic spot. From there Wolfe found it possible to shell the town and protect the ships of the fleet as they sailed up the river past the French guns. Whether or not he captured the city, he could now bombard it into ruin.

His bad stroke—his darkest day—came at the end of July when he attacked the northern shore in force between the town and Montmorency Cataract. At water level the French had two gun emplacements. In front of this battery were mud flats, as much as a half mile wide when the tide was out; behind it were almost vertical cliffs, with the bulk of Montcalm's army at the top. What Wolfe expected to accomplish, how he planned to get up the cliffs, is not clear.

His men landed on a sultry afternoon, slogged through mud and slime to capture the battery, and then in a kind of contagious madness, started for the cliffs. They were easy targets. Even as they clawed their way upward, clutching at branches and crevices, a thunderstorm drenched their powder and sent them slithering down among the rocks. In that point-blank slaughter 440 English were killed or wounded, while not a Frenchman died. As the English rowed away, leaving behind the twisted bodies of their comrades on the beach, the Indians crept down the cliff with their scalping knives.

There was only one way, Wolfe finally realized, to take Quebec, and that was to attack the town itself. Montcalm, with his mixed militia army, would not be foolish enough to come down from the heights and give

battle. He would wait for General Winter to do that. Already Wolfe could see the first burnish on the maple trees, and the fear of returning to England without Quebec grew on him. At his generals' urging he determined to test the defenses above the city rather than below it. With each favoring evening tide Admiral Saunders now slipped a ship or two past the French guns until he had assembled a fleet of more than twenty vessels above the town.

By now the number of men in Wolfe's army fit for duty was only half what it had been on his arrival. He himself was ailing and sensed that he had not long to live. "I know you cannot cure my complaint," he told the army surgeon, "but patch me up so that I may be able to do my duty for the next few days and I shall be content."

By September 6 he had 3,600 men aboard the flotilla above the town. His problem now was how to land his army and get it up the forbidding cliffs without inviting another slaughter like the one at Montmorency. Upriver the English ships drifted with each incoming tide, and back they came again as the tide ebbed. The Canadian militia followed along the cliff top, keeping

Montreal, seen from across the St. Lawrence, looked like this in 1760. The second city of Canada, it was a major objective.

abreast of the ships. For a week the ships drifted with the current, the redcoats on board cramped, seasick, and grumbling. Wolfe made no attempt to land.

Yet he had at last found what he was looking for—a way leading to the heights. Somehow he discovered that about a mile and a half above the town, at an inlet known ever afterward as Wolfe's Cove, an obscure path wound up the cliff. The summit there was guarded by only a squad of militia.

Wolfe finally set September 13 for his landing attempt. It was just the right night, dark and calm and moonless. The flotilla drifted some six miles beyond Wolfe's Cove and then waited for the tide to reverse. At midnight the troops began to shift from the transports into the whaleboats. Two hours later the ebb tide commenced, and a shrouded lantern was hung as a signal from the leading ship.

The packed whaleboats cast off, drifting downstream slowly, followed by reserves and artillery and finally by the remaining ships. The advance boats glided silently, the oars scarcely breaking the reflection of the autumn stars. Wedged together, the men hardly spoke to one another, their minds withdrawn into that mixture of fear, excitement, and impatience that soldiers always feel just before action. As they slipped into the shadow near the shore they could make out the heavier shadows of the cliffs.

Suddenly, close to the cove, a sentry's voice rang out: *"Qui vive!"* A young officer of the 78th Highlanders who spoke French answered back in a low hoarse voice, "France! Long live the King!" Then the current carried them safely around a headland, and Wolfe's Cove lay in front of them.

Wolfe was among the first to land. As he gave orders and the initial detachment started climbing, the looming cliff seemed too formidable to him. The men were too engrossed and the going was too rough for them to think such thoughts. For all their efforts at quietness they stumbled and fell and cursed; branches snapped; canteens clanked against boulders; dislodged rocks rattled downhill. To the breathless, anxious soldiers it seemed that they had given themselves away a dozen times, but still there was no sound from the enemy. Not until the first English reached the summit and over-powered the panicky French militiamen was a shot fired. But the way was now secured and the rest of the army could follow. As the darkness ebbed, the wan morning light showed hundreds of redcoats swarming up the cliff. The French batteries from Quebec opened up in alarm, and the guns from the frigates returned the fire.

As soon as the English regiments reached the heights, Wolfe formed them up on the plateau above the town known as the Plains of Abraham. Here at last he could fight a battle in the grand manner, as European generals had always felt a battle should be fought: row on row of regular infantry advancing rigidly with the iron discipline of which the Indians and the militia-men were incapable. Soon after dawn it began to drizzle. At about six the English front ranks caught their first glimpse of the enemy's white uniforms. The redcoats continued to stand motionless in the thin rain, their regimental flags hanging damply.

Montcalm had hurried out from the town as soon as he was told the news. When he finally saw the challeng-ing red lines and heard the drone of the bagpipes, he knew his hour of decision had come. With only five regular regiments he was outnumbered slightly, but he had no choice. The British were astride Quebec's sup-ply line, and its landward fortifications were too weak to withstand a siege. A quarter of a mile away he formed up his army with Indians and Canadians on the flanks.

As the waiting minutes ticked off, Wolfe walked up and down the ranks, talking cheerfully to his men, ignoring the sharpshooters' bullets that now began to buzz like hornets. He was an obvious target. Before long a bullet cut through his wrist, tearing the tendons, but he had an aide tie it with a handkerchief and continued as if nothing had happened.

The rain stopped and the sun slipped out. The day grew warm. Montcalm, in a green and gold uniform, rode up and down his line encouraging his own men. He looked sad and tired. In contrast, Wolfe's pale face shone with a stiff, radiant happiness.

At ten o'clock the French drums began to beat, and the army began moving with slow deliberation toward the waiting English five hundred yards away. The white line marched six deep, each soldier four feet from the next. Though the drums echoed more threateningly, the English line remained unmoving. At 150 yards the French quickened their pace and began to fire raggedly. Still the English stood, without returning a shot. When a redcoat dropped, the ranks closed. A corporal remembered afterward how he could even see the buttons on the Frenchmen's coats. Fifty yards away, then forty, and Wolfe himself gave the order to fire.

It was a shattering volley with a report like a roll of thunder as unit after unit fired. Stoically, as if they were drilling, the redcoats reloaded, advanced twenty paces, and fired again. It was more than the French could bear. All down their line lay the bodies of the dead and the writhing wounded. The unnerved survivors broke and began to run back to the town. Wolfe gave the order to charge, and the redcoats dashed forward with their bayonets while the Highlanders dropped their

122

guns and swung their broadswords. The battle became a rout.

Wolfe, hurrying ahead, staggered and fell, shot through the lungs. The red-haired commander tried to get to his feet, but this time he knew the end had come. "Now God be praised," he whispered to the soldier who held him. "Since I have conquered I will die in peace."

Montcalm, forced back by his panicky soldiers, was struck in the chest by an exploding shell near the Quebec gates. He had two soldiers hold him in his saddle so that the men could not see how badly he was hurt. Some hours later he died and was buried secretly in a shell hole in the chapel of the Ursuline Convent. By evening the French army had abandoned the town.

Wolfe's victory on the Plains of Abraham was one of the fateful battles in history and certainly the most important of the French and Indian Wars. The struggle would run on for another year, even after the decisive battle, but the hopes of New France were buried with Montcalm.

After his capture of Ticonderoga and Crown Point, Amherst, had he been a man of Wolfe's temperament, might have thrust for Montreal and ended the war by winter. William Johnson and General Prideaux, who was killed in the effort, had taken the French forts at Oswego and Niagara. Instead, the Cautious Commander preferred to play it safe. The following summer he advanced three armies on Montreal: from Quebec, from Crown Point, and from the west. In a brilliant military maneuver they joined almost simultaneously before the island town. Governor Vaudreuil was forced to surrender. The seventy-year war had at last come to an end.

Yet wars, when they end, have a way of being only a beginning. France had lost her New World empire. Never again would the Indians hold the shifting balance between two sides. For the colonists the long nightmare of ambush and attack was over. The Great Lakes and the West lay open to the bold. In the moment of victory the transplanted Englishmen felt a renewed affection for the mother country. There was no shadow yet over England's American empire, fated in so few years to follow the French in eclipse. Now Amherst appeared a hero in America, and the colonies rejoiced too at the accession of the young king, George III, as popular at first as he was later unpopular. Such was the mood—and so brief. Within a decade the mother country would become the ugly stepmother, and the redcoats that had been a symbol of protection would seem a symbol of tyranny.

There were a few cold-blooded politicians in England who would have given Canada back to France in exchange for some sugar island, cynically feeling that the French threat was necessary to keep the colonists from developing ideas of independence. But their second thoughts came too late. A page of history had been turned.

FOR FURTHER READING

*Cooper, James Fenimore. *The Deerslayer*. Scribner's, 1953.

*Cooper, James Fenimore. *The Last of the Mohicans*. Scribner's, 1952.

Cuneo, John R. *Robert Rogers of the Rangers*. Oxford University Press, 1959.

Eccles, W. J. *Frontenac—The Courtier Governor*. McClelland and Stuart Ltd., 1959.

*Edmonds, Walter D. *Drums Along the Mohawk*. Little, Brown, 1936.

Flexner, James T. *Mohawk Baronet: Sir William Johnson of New York*. Harper, 1959.

James, Alfred P. *Drums in the Forest*. Historical Society of Western Pennsylvania, 1958.

Lancaster, Bruce. *Ticonderoga—the Story of a Fort*. Houghton Mifflin, 1959.

Lenski, Lois. *Indian Captive: The Story of Mary Jemison*. Lippincott, 1941.

Lounsberry, Alice. *Sir William Phips*. Scribner's, 1941.

McCardell, Lee. *Ill-Starred General: Braddock of the Coldstream Guards*. University of Pittsburgh Press, 1958.

Parkman, Francis. *The Battle for North America*. (Abridged and edited by John Tebbel.) Doubleday, 1948.

Peckham, Howard. *Captured by Indians*. Rutgers University Press, 1954.

Pound, Arthur. *Lake Ontario*. Bobbs-Merrill, 1945.

*Roberts, Kenneth L. *Northwest Passage*. Doubleday, 1959.

Rutledge, Joseph L. *Century of Conflict*. Doubleday, 1956.

Stacey, C. P. *Quebec, 1759*. Macmillan, 1959.

Toye, William. *The St. Lawrence*. Henry Z. Walck, 1959.

Van de Water, Frederick W. *Lake Champlain and Lake George*. Bobbs-Merrill, 1946.

Wellman, Paul I. *Indian Wars and Warriors*. Houghton Mifflin, 1959.

*Fiction

Benjamin West's painting of Wolfe's death at his moment of triumph, inaccurate and romanticized as it may be, still captures the dramatic and somber grandeur of this battle climaxing the seventy-year struggle for North America.

INDEX

127